ST. TERESA
OF AVILA

"If any man will come after me, let him deny himself, and take up his cross, and follow me. For he that will save his life, shall lose it: and he that shall lose his life for my sake, shall find it."

—Matthew 16:24-25

St. Teresa of Jesus,
also known as St. Teresa of Avila

ST. TERESA OF AVILA

1515-1582

REFORMER OF CARMEL

By

F. A. Forbes

"And every one that hath left house, or brethren, or sisters, or father, or mother, or wife, or children, or lands for my name's sake, shall receive an hundredfold, and shall possess life everlasting."
—Matthew 19:29

TAN BOOKS AND PUBLISHERS, INC.
Rockford, Illinois 61105

Nihil Obstat: Francis M. Canon Wyndham
　　　　　　　Censor Deputatus

Imprimatur:　Edmund Canon Surmont
　　　　　　　Vicar General
　　　　　　　Westminster
　　　　　　　August 10, 1917

Originally published in 1917 by R. & T. Washbourne, Ltd., London, as *The Life of Saint Teresa* in the series *Standard-bearers of the Faith: A Series of Lives of the Saints for Young and Old.*

ISBN 0-89555-625-1

Library of Congress Catalog Card No.: 98-61410

Cover and frontispiece illustration: St. Teresa of Jesus, by Alonso del Arco (17th century). M. Lázaro Galdeano, Madrid.

Printed and bound in the United States of America.

TAN BOOKS AND PUBLISHERS, INC.
P.O. Box 424
Rockford, Illinois 61105
1998

"He who in the heights is the Lord, in the depths is the Beloved; above the stars He reigns; among the lilies He loves."

—St. Bernard

CONTENTS

St. Teresa of Avila

Ribera

Chapter 1

GIRLHOOD

> "He who loves Thee, O my God, travels safely by the open and royal road, far from the precipice; he has scarcely stumbled at all when Thou stretchest forth Thy hand to save him."
> —*St. Teresa*

"IT was the little girl who made me do it," pleaded Rodrigo de Cepeda, and although he did not know it, the excuse was as old as the world.

The "little girl" in question was Rodrigo's seven-year-old sister Teresa, who had been seized with a burning desire for martyrdom. She wanted to see God, she passionately assured her brother, and as it was necessary to die first, martyrdom was obviously the only means to her end. Rodrigo himself had not seen the matter quite in the same light, but as Teresa was his own particular friend and playmate, and they had always done everything together, he had considered himself bound to enter into her views.

The two had set forth hand in hand at an

1

early hour in the morning to seek the desired martyrdom in the country of the Moors, but fate had been against them. Scarcely had the children left the town of Avila when they fell into the hands of an uncle, who was returning from the country. Untouched by their tears and prayers, he promptly took them home, to the relief of the anxious mother, who was searching everywhere for the missing pair. Rodrigo's excuse has already been given. Teresa with earnest eyes repeated her assertion: "I wanted to go to God, and one cannot do that unless one dies first."

Doña Beatriz de Ahumada was a wise and saintly woman. She explained gently to her little daughter that for most people the road to God lies through a life spent faithfully in His service. Such a life, especially if one tried one's best to please God in everything one did and was careful to avoid offending Him, might be quite as meritorious as the shorter way of martyrdom, which was, moreover, only for the few.

It was hard to give up all one's dreams. Teresa consulted the Lives of the Saints and decided that the most desirable thing, after a martyr's death, was a hermit's life. Assisted by the faithful Rodrigo, she set to work to build a hermitage in the garden, but, as cement had not entered into their plans, the stones fell down as fast as they built them up. Teresa was at last obliged to admit sorrowfully that there seemed no more prospect of a hermit's life than of a martyr's death, and it was in this moment of discouragement that her mother's words came back to her. To do one's best to please God and not to offend Him seemed possible for anybody; she determined, therefore, to try this simple plan and with her usual energy set to work at once.

She had not very much pocket-money, but what she had she gave to the poor; she tried to say her prayers as devoutly as possible and resolved to do a kind action or say a kind word to everyone she met. It sounds like a simple program, but it took the little girl all her time and cost her many acts of self-denial—how many, those who practice it will soon discover. But she brought sunshine with her wherever she went, and she began to be supremely happy, for there is no joy like that of giving joy to others.

Doña Beatriz de Ahumada, Teresa's sweet young mother, did her utmost to bring up her large family in the fear and the love of God. Gentle, pure and devout, she was herself their best example. Of the three sisters and nine brothers who made up the merry family party in the big house at Avila, not one in later life lost the strong faith and fervor that had been so firmly rooted in their childish hearts. Don Alonso de Cepeda, her husband, was a man whom all respected.

Truthful, charitable and chivalrous, he was loved as well as obeyed by all his children. St. Teresa herself tells us that she never knew her father or mother to respect anything but goodness and that all the children in mind and heart took after their parents. "All, that is," she adds in her humility, "but myself."

The happy family life was soon to be broken up. When Teresa was between twelve and thirteen years old, Doña Beatriz died. In the anguish of loneliness that followed the loss of the mother to whom she had confided all her joys and sorrows, the child flung herself on her knees before the Blessed Virgin, begging her to be her mother now that she no longer had one on earth.

Of all the family, Teresa was perhaps the one who missed Doña Beatriz the most sorely and needed her guiding hand the most. Maria, her elder sister, was already grown up; Juana, the younger, scarcely more than a baby; Teresa, beautiful, brilliant and lovable, was just growing from childhood into girlhood. Her brothers adored her, and among the troop of young cousins who frequented the house she ruled as a little queen. There was no danger as long as Teresa carried out her resolution of pleasing God and never offending Him; but time wore on, and she who had inspired that resolution was no longer at hand to encourage and advise.

The apparition of the Holy Child to St. Teresa.

5

There was one among Teresa's cousins, a good deal older than herself, whose conversation, she tells us, did her much harm. She was a shallow and frivolous girl who thought of nothing but pleasure and amusement. By the time Teresa was fourteen, she seemed to have forgotten all her old desires of being a Saint. Whatever time could be spared from the reading of romances was spent in setting off her girlish beauty to the best advantage and enjoying the admiration that she received from all within the little home circle.

But the Blessed Virgin did not forget the child who had thrown herself at her feet on the day of her mother's death. Though Teresa was her father's darling, he was not so blinded by affection for his young daughter as not to notice the change in her behavior. He was the first to see that her prayers were more hurried, her visits to the church fewer; that she thought more of herself and less of others. He noticed with distress the unworthy friendship that was doing all the mischief. He noticed, too, that in spite of all her amusements, Teresa was less joyous than of old when she had set her childish steps to "go to God."

He took counsel with his eldest daughter, Maria, who had also remarked the change in her sister and was grieving over it in silence. She herself was soon to be married, and it was this that helped them to come to a decision, for when Maria was established in a house of her own, Teresa could not very well remain at home alone with her brothers. It was decided to send her to the Augustinian Convent to complete her education, and no sooner was the wedding over than the plan was carried out.

After the first week or two of homesickness, Teresa was heartily glad. She was already tired of the life she had been leading, and the old desires were tugging at her heartstrings. Sister Maria Briceño, the nun who was the mistress of the secular children at the convent, helped a great deal to set Teresa on the path to sanctity. It was she who opened Teresa's mind, by her holy example and advice, to the possibility of becoming a nun.

Teresa remained a year and a half at the convent in the company of this holy nun. Then, however, she became seriously ill and had to return to her father's house. When Teresa's strength was somewhat recovered, she and her father, Don Alonso, set out for Castellanos de la Canada, the home of Teresa's sister Maria. On the road lay the home of Don Pedro, Teresa's uncle, a holy old man who lived the life of a recluse and a Saint in Hortigosa. Don Alonso's stay could only be short, as he was obliged to return home on business, but Don Pedro was

so delighted with Teresa that he begged his
brother to leave her with him until he could
come back and fetch her home himself a week
or two later.

Hortigosa seemed a little dull to Teresa after
the happy life she had led with her sister until
Don Pedro, the greater part of whose time was
passed in prayer and study, proposed one day
that his niece should read aloud to him in her
spare moments. Teresa, always ready to give pleasure to others, set herself bravely to a task which
she did not expect to enjoy. To her surprise,
however, the Epistles of St. Jerome and the writ-
ings of St. Augustine and St. Gregory, which
were what her uncle chiefly preferred, turned
out to be less dry than she had expected. Her
quick intelligence and love of all that was noble
and beautiful soon made her almost as eager for
the hour of reading as Don Pedro himself, and
many were the happy moments spent in the old
Spanish garden at Hortigosa.

As the time went on, Don Pedro and his
young niece found that they had much in common. They talked now over the daily reading,
while the old desire to seek and to find God
arose more strongly than ever in Teresa's heart,
with a deeper understanding of the means to be
taken. Already she had discovered that earthly
pleasures were unsatisfying. She had learned that

those who give the most to God are the happiest, and yet her nature shrank, as human nature will, from sacrifice and suffering. How was it all to end? That was the question uppermost in Teresa's heart when her father came to take her home to Avila.

Chapter 2

THE CALL OF GOD

"Let him begin by not being afraid of the Cross, and he will see how Our Lord will help him to carry it." —*St. Teresa*

TERESA was courageous by nature, and the long talks with her uncle in the garden at Hortigosa had reawakened all the desires of her childhood. A long life of experience had taught the old man what the child had learned by intuition, that "to get to God" was the one thing in the world worth striving for.

What was the surest way to Paradise? was the question Teresa asked herself. In spite of the fact that her nature shrank from the thought of the religious life with all that it entailed of self-sacrifice, she earnestly prayed that God would show her what He desired of her and that He would give her the strength to do it. How would it be for her in the future if she remained in the world? She had been weak once already in the presence of danger.

10

That the religious life was the highest life she was certain; she soon became convinced that for her at least it was the safest. As for its hardships, its self-denial, if other people had borne them, why not she? Could she not suffer a little for that Lord who had suffered so much for her? And after all, was not He Himself the strength of those who chose the rough ways for His sake?

So it was, in quiet communing with her own soul, weighing the things of earth against the things of Heaven, that Teresa chose the latter, with all that the sacrifice entailed. It remained to break the news to her father. That he would suffer Teresa knew, but, once assured that her resolve was taken, she had no doubt but that he would give her generously to God.

In this, however, she was mistaken. Don Alonso absolutely refused his consent. Entreaties were of no avail; arguments could not move him. In vain Teresa appealed to her sister Maria, to her uncle, Don Pedro; in vain her brothers, touched by her evident distress, pleaded her cause with their father. Teresa was his favorite child, said Don Alonso; he could not and would not part with her. He wished to hear no more of the matter.

But if Don Alonso was resolute, Teresa was resolute too, for God had spoken, and she saw

St. Teresa as a young girl entering the monastery.

clearly where her duty lay. Although her heart was breaking at the thought of parting from those she loved so dearly and the home life that was so sweet, she determined to take things into her own hands.

Close to the town of Avila, in the midst of its quiet gardens, lay the Carmelite Convent of the Incarnation. Thither a few years before Juana Suarez, a beloved friend of Teresa's, had gone to give her young life to God in the cloister. From her Teresa had learned something of the peace and happiness of the religious life, and the prayers of Juana and of her sisters in religion had been enlisted to win Don Alonso's consent.

One of Teresa's brothers—not the faithful Rodrigo, who was already making a military career for himself in the New World, but Antonio—showed her much sympathy, for the desire of his heart also was to belong to God. Brother and sister at last resolved to leave their father's house together and to enter religion, Teresa at the Incarnation and Antonio at the Dominican monastery nearby.

Early in the morning, before the household was astir, as in the old days when Teresa had crept out with Rodrigo to seek martyrdom in the country of the Moors, the two set forth. Teresa herself tells us that the agony she felt at leaving the beloved home of her childhood was so great that she did not think the pains of death could be greater, but not for that would she pause.

Once within the convent walls a deep peace fell on her soul. On that very day, as was the custom, her beautiful hair was cut off and she was clothed with the novice's habit and veil. Kneeling before the Tabernacle, she thanked God who had given her the strength to do what she knew was His Will and offered herself to Him forever. A few days later her happiness was complete, for Don Alonso, who had been thinking things over in his heart, came himself to the Convent of the Incarnation to give his daughter the consent that he had so long withheld.

The bond between the two was now deeper and stronger than ever, ennobled as it was by sacrifice. Humbly Don Alonso asked Teresa to teach him, now that she herself had chosen the higher life, how to serve God better. The parlor of the Incarnation became for him and for Teresa's brothers the sunniest spot in Avila. There each one brought his troubles and difficulties; careers were decided on and plans discussed for the future; the bright young novice had help and advice for all. Even Antonio would come from time to time from his monastery to talk about the spiritual life with the sister who had helped him so much to understand its meaning

during their last days at home together. As for
the little Juana, Don Alonso brought her himself to the convent, that her education might be
carried on under Teresa's care.

If the struggle was still sometimes keen in the
novice's heart, no one was allowed to suspect it.
She performed her humble duties with such a
radiant face that everyone who saw her was
cheered by the sight. She prayed with so much
fervor and atoned for her mistakes with so much
humility that her sisters used sometimes to wonder what the little novice would become in later
life. Her greatest joy was in helping others. She
was always on the look-out for such little opportunities, but the old and the infirm were her
special care.

When Teresa knelt at her bedside at night, if
her chances of practicing charity throughout the
day had been few, she would grieve over it and
ask God's pardon. Sometimes it would happen
at that very moment that an uncertain footfall
would pass her door, and she would know that
in the darkness one of the sisters was groping
her way to her cell. Then Teresa would spring
up, and, taking a little lamp in her hand, has-
ten to light her on her way, rejoicing that God
had sent her the chance of doing one more kind
action before she slept.

So highly was her thoughtfulness for others

appreciated that she was named to help in the infirmary, an employment usually given to the professed alone. She loved the sick, and they loved her. They knew that they could ask any service of her, and that she was never weary of waiting on them, however tiring and unpleasant to her nature the duties might be. There was one among them who suffered from a terrible disease and whose poor body was a mass of open sores. Teresa, who knew that many of the sisters, in spite of themselves, shrank from approaching her, made herself her special nurse. Not content with dressing the gaping wounds, she would sit beside her patient by the hour, kiss her hands and do everything she could to show that, far from being a mortification to serve her, it was her greatest joy. Filled with admiration at the courage and resignation with which the sufferer bore her terrible malady, Teresa would ask God that if ever she herself should be attacked with illness, she might have grace to bear it with the same love and patience.

It seemed as if God had heard her prayer, for not long after Teresa herself began to fail in health. At first she took no notice of the continual sickness and weariness that assailed her, for she was not given to thinking about her own ailments. The day of her profession was drawing nigh, and everything else was forgotten in the thought that she would soon belong wholly to Our Lord.

But the happy day came and passed, and Teresa grew rather worse than better. Her superiors took alarm; treatment after treatment was tried, but in vain. It was now her turn to accept the services of others and to practice patience. The days and nights in the infirmary were long for one so young and normally so full of life and energy. The dear community life of work and prayer that she loved so much had to be given up; she was too weak even to read.

Yet, as Teresa lay helpless on her bed and contrasted the old happy days with the present time of suffering, there were no complaints, even in her own heart. "Since I have received good things from my Lord," she would say gently, "why not also evil?" Her sisters were touched at the sight of the cheerful content that never seemed to waver. As of old, she thought of others more than of herself and did her best to give as little trouble as possible.

Don Alonso, in great distress, sent physician after physician to see his daughter, but all declared that nothing could be done; the illness was incurable. At last, in despair, he resolved to take her to a woman doctor who had a reputation for working wonderful cures. The nuns of the Convent of the Incarnation were not cloistered but were allowed to go and visit their intimate friends and relations; there would be therefore no difficulty in taking Teresa to Bézédas, where the woman lived. Juana Suarez, the friend of Teresa's girlhood, was permitted to go with her, for the nuns were anxious to do all they could for one whom they felt certain they would never see again.

In the early winter the three set out together for Hortigosa, the first stage on their journey. The treatment was not to begin until the spring, but Don Alonso had planned that Teresa should spend the winter months with her sister Maria. Since the air of Castellanos had done her so much good before, who could tell what it might not do again? At all events, it was worth trying.

Chapter 3

THE GREAT MISTAKE

"They who would follow Christ, if they do
not wish to be lost, must walk in the way He
walked Himself."   —St. Teresa

IF Don Pedro was delighted to see his niece
clothed in the religious habit, he was no less
distressed at her condition. He surrounded her
with every care during her short stay at Hortigosa, and the little book on prayer which he
gave her as a parting gift soon became Teresa's
chief treasure. The long hours of suffering and
weakness, during which she could neither work
nor read, she resolved to spend in a union with
God which should be closer than ever. It was
the only way, as she had learned by experience,
to be cheerful and patient when in continual
pain. Now, with the help of her uncle's little
book, she set to work to make prayer the chief
occupation of her life.

She used to try, Teresa tells us, to imagine
Jesus Christ her Lord present within her soul,

and with a loving heart to follow Him through all the mysteries of His earthly life, praying the while that she might serve Him to the utmost of her power. Her father and sister, knowing that she now belonged to God and not to them, were careful not to disturb her; but if they were thoughtful of her, she too was thoughtful of them. When they were with her, no matter how much she might be suffering, she was always gay and merry, and the greatest treat for Maria's two little children was to be allowed to visit their aunt.

So the months wore on; but to Don Alonso's grief, Teresa grew no better. The air of Castellanos, that was to work such marvels, seemed to have lost its magic. When the early spring arrived and it was time to set out for Bézédas, the journey had to be taken more slowly than ever, for Teresa was so weak that even the most careful movement brought on alarming fainting fits. The quack doctor from whose skill Don Alonso had hoped so much turned out to be an ignorant woman, whose violent remedies were utterly unsuited to anyone in Teresa's condition. Under her treatment the invalid lost the last remnants of strength that she possessed. Racked with pain from head to foot, burning with fever and wasted to a skeleton, she was brought back to Avila by her heartbroken father in a condition more dead than alive.

It was the Vigil of the Assumption, and Teresa wished to make her Confession. Her eagerness, however, alarmed Don Alonso, who feared that it might be prompted by the thought that she was dying. In order, as he imagined, to reassure her and to convince her that there was no real danger, he refused to send for a priest. That very night Teresa became unconscious and remained thus for four days. It was reported in the town that she was dead; her grave was dug at the Convent of the Incarnation, and two sisters were sent to watch by her coffin. Don Alonso alone refused to give up hope, even when the doctor despaired. Reproaching himself bitterly for his refusal to grant Teresa's last desire, he knelt night and day by her bedside, chafing her cold hands in his and beseeching God that she might not die without the Sacraments, through his fault. His prayer was granted. On the fourth day Teresa opened her eyes, smiled at her father and her brothers, who were gathered round her bed, and repeated her request. This time the poor father did not hesitate; the priest was sent for at once.

Teresa made her Confession and received her Lord with tears of joy, after which the cruel sufferings, for a moment interrupted, began again more violently than ever. For nearly seven months she lay in agony, expressing only one desire—

to return to her convent. Don Alonso at last yielded to her wish, and she was transported with the greatest care to the Incarnation, an object of pity to all who beheld her. For eight months more she remained unable to move, at the end of which time, to her great joy, she was able to crawl about on her hands and knees.

During these weary days of suffering and helplessness, prayer was her one comfort and charity her only thought. It was said that in her presence the absent were always safe, for she would allow nothing to be said against them. Her cheerful patience astonished her sisters; they could not understand how it could endure amid such sufferings. A talk with her was like a tonic for those who were in difficulties or sad at heart.

The doctors had decided that the paralysis was incurable; but to the young nun of twenty-four, who had already suffered so much and who lay looking forward to a life of helpless inaction, there came a great longing to work for Our Lord as well as to suffer for Him. Earthly doctors had failed her; she would appeal to the heavenly. She had always had a great devotion to St. Joseph, and it was to him she now addressed herself. "To other Saints," she wrote in later life, "Our Lord seems to have given grace to succor men in some special necessity, but to this glorious Saint, I know by experience, to help us in all.

He helps in a special way those souls who commend themselves to him."

The answer to her prayer was a complete cure.

Teresa had asked for health that she might serve God better, and He had granted her request. The time had come to put into practice all that had been planned during the hours of prayer and suffering.

Looking back on the past in later years, Teresa declared that she had been wrong in thinking that she could serve God better in health than in sickness. "He knows what is for our good," she says, "and His Holy Will is best." For in spite of all her desires, sixteen years were to pass before, leaving the things of earth behind her, she was to reach those heights of holiness to which God had called her.

The Rule of the Order of Mount Carmel, drawn up by St. Albert, Patriarch of Jerusalem, on a foundation much older still, prescribed silence, solitude, prayer and perpetual abstinence from meat. Toward the end of the fourteenth century, when the Great Schism had brought with it a relaxation of the religious orders, men began to grow weary of austerity, and the Carmelites obtained from the Pope a mitigation or softening of their Rule. The severe fasts and abstinences were done away with, enclosure was given up and the spirit of prayer that had been the characteristic of the Order rapidly declined.

The Convent of the Incarnation had been founded lately under the mitigated Rule; the nuns knew no other. They led good, holy lives, but not very different from those which they might have led as good Catholics in the world. Visitors were allowed at all hours, the religious were permitted to leave the convent to stay with friends and relations, silence was not observed and abstinence from meat not practiced. The friends and families of the nuns availed themselves largely of their opportunities and frequented the parlors and the garden of the convent.

Teresa, warm of heart and affectionate by nature, could not refuse to receive the many visitors who flocked to see her on her recovery, conscious though she was that such visits did not tend to a spirit of prayer and recollection. People declared that she did them good and helped them, which was undoubtedly true, for she had the gift of leading souls to God. Other nuns whose virtue she admired did the same thing, she argued to herself; it was the custom of the convent. But all souls are not called to the same perfection, and the results soon made themselves felt in Teresa's spiritual life. The prayer and union with God which she had practiced in the infirmary began to be impossible under these new conditions, amid the distractions caused

by these incessant visits. Teresa began to think
that it would be better for her, imperfect as she
was, to content herself with the vocal prayers
prescribed by the Rule. Why should she aspire
to a closer union with God than those among
whom she lived?

Yet she could not be at rest, for the voice of
God spoke continually in her soul, urging her
to be faithful to her earlier aspirations. Although
a faithful and fervent religious in the eyes of all,
Teresa knew in her own heart how far she fell
short of the perfection to which God was call-
ing her. Neither was she without warning, for
one day when talking with a friend whose
acquaintance she had lately made, she became
suddenly aware of a horrible toad-like creature
crawling rapidly toward her. On another occasion while she was with the same person, Our
Lord appeared to her, His sad and reproachful
face haunting her for long days afterward.

Don Alonso, who had taken to heart Teresa's
instructions of earlier days, was advancing rapidly
in the way of prayer and holiness. Smitten to
the heart by the veneration with which he
regarded her, Teresa told him that she no longer
prayed as of old, but she did not disturb him
in his belief that it was her health, which was
still far from good, that prevented her. She little knew that the death of her beloved father

was to be the beginning of her own new life. Suddenly struck down with a dangerous illness, he sent an imploring message to his best-beloved daughter to come to his bedside. Teresa, with the permission of her superiors, hastened to give him the comfort he desired. Though in great pain, the holy old man thought only of his soul and of the life to come and bore his sufferings with heroic patience.

The end was near, and it was at her father's deathbed that Teresa found courage for the fight. She had been much struck by the fervor and piety of the Dominican friar who had assisted Don Alonso in his last hours, and she determined to have recourse to him for the needs of her own soul. He understood at once to what heights God had called her. In the first place, he told her, she must hold fast to mental prayer and under no condition give it up.

Teresa obeyed; but it was hard to preserve the recollection necessary for that intimate communion with God in the midst of the distractions to which the relations with her numerous friends exposed her. For years the conflict raged in her soul. She had not the strength to give up her friendships, although she felt that God desired that of her. The hours of prayer were hours of anguish, sometimes spent in a frenzied longing for the clock to strike, sometimes in tears and

contrition at the thought of her own weakness.
Teresa was nearly forty years old when the grace
of God at last triumphed in her soul.

Chapter 4

CHRIST OR SATAN?

"O Life of all lives, Thou slayest none that put their trust in Thee and seek Thy friendship."
— *St. Teresa*

IT has been said that God will never allow Himself to be outdone in generosity. For fourteen years, in spite of dryness, weariness and ill health, Teresa persevered in prayer. After a long struggle, very hard to her affectionate nature, she had given up all the earthly ties to which she clung. The reward followed closely on the sacrifice. God began to reveal Himself to her soul with an ever-increasing intimacy, while the sense of His continual presence never left her. It was no longer hard to recollect herself; the thought of God was always in her heart. Her soul, as she herself tells us, lost itself in God; she no longer lived, but God lived in her.

It was about this time that St. Francis Borgia, General of the Spanish Province of the Jesuits, resolved to found a Jesuit College in Avila.

Rumors of the holiness of the two sons of St. Ignatius who had been sent there to inaugurate the work came to the ears of Teresa, who conceived an ardent desire to seek their counsel and advice. The very graces which God was showering upon her made her uneasy. In her humility she asked herself if she, a sinner, were not unworthy of such favors, and she feared lest the devil might be deceiving her.

Teresa had some reasons for her misgivings. Not long before, the visions and prophecies of a certain Franciscan nun of Cordova had been the wonder and admiration of the whole country. After having been regarded as a Saint for thirty years, this woman, suddenly touched by grace, had confessed that her life had been a deception and her visions imaginary, and she was now expiating her sins in bitter sorrow in a convent of her Order. If one nun could be so deceived, thought Teresa, why not another? Convinced as she was of her own unworthiness, the extraordinary graces which God had vouchsafed to her only served to alarm her.

Teresa had heard that the Jesuits were remarkable for their wisdom and skill in the guidance of souls and she longed to have recourse to them to set her doubts at rest. But humility interfered once more. "I did not think myself fit to speak to them," says the Saint, and the desire had to await its fulfillment. There lived in Avila a holy old man who was dear to Teresa, not only on account of the purity of his life, but because he had been the intimate friend of her father. His name was Don Francisco de Salcedo, and to him Teresa resolved to confide her difficulty. Having heard her to the end, he proposed that she should submit the case to Doctor Gaspar Daza, a learned theologian and a friend of his own.

The interview which resulted was not very satisfactory. Dr. Daza had not time to undertake the direction of the Saint and could only give her some general advice, while Teresa, who had not as yet that understanding of spiritual things which was to be her characteristic in later years, found great difficulty in making her explanation clear. An internal intuition, moreover, told her that this was not the man to help her.

Don Francisco, greatly disappointed at the failure of his enterprise, did his best to console her and suggested that she should write an account of her spiritual experiences for Dr. Daza to read. This, to the best of her ability, she did, and gave the manuscript to her old friend. The consequences were disastrous; Don Francisco returned in the greatest distress. Dr. Daza had read her account, he told her, and had come to the conclusion, in which he himself was obliged to concur, that her consolations were the work of the evil one. The best thing for her to do would be to put herself immediately under the direction of a Jesuit.

Teresa was heartbroken; she did not even dare to pray, for fear that the consolation she might receive would be of the devil, and Father de Padranos was asked to come at once to the convent to hear her Confession.

To the Jesuit the situation was perfectly clear: he saw the grace of God working in a soul that was pure, humble and straightforward. What was going on in her, he said, was the work of the Spirit of God; she was destined for great graces and must do all in her power to correspond with them. She was to abandon herself with trust and confidence wholly into God's hands.

Teresa breathed again; anguish was succeeded by peace and joy, but her doubts were to be still further set at rest. St. Francis Borgia, the General of the Jesuits, came soon afterward to Avila to visit the College of St. Giles, and at Father de Padranos' request went to the Incarnation to see her. The Spirit of God was leading her, was his verdict; she might safely follow Its guidance. Unfortunately for Teresa's future peace of mind, Father Juan de Padranos was shortly afterward called away from Avila.

Meanwhile, the number of nuns in the Convent of the Incarnation was increasing rapidly.

Finances did not increase at the same rate, hence it was difficult to keep up the house without continually appealing to the families of the nuns for help. In order to relieve the convent of the increasing burden, the sisters were encouraged more and more to visit their friends and relations and were even ordered to accept all invitations.

Teresa deplored the want of enclosure with all her heart. Nothing was more contrary to her inclinations than such visiting; but it was the custom of the house, and she was obliged to obey. While staying with one of her cousins she had made the acquaintance of Doña Guiomar de Ulloa, a young widow of twenty-five who, having lately lost her husband, had resolved to seek consolation in God alone. Attracted by Teresa's charm of manner no less than by her holiness, Doña Guiomar had confided to her her hopes and fears for the future, and a strong and supernatural friendship had arisen between them. When the Saint returned to her convent it was only to hear that Doña Guiomar had sought and obtained permission to invite her to her own house a few months later.

When the two friends met Teresa was struck once more by the progress that Doña Guiomar had made in the spiritual life. It was entirely owing, she explained later, to the direction of

Father Baltasar Alvarez, a young Jesuit whose holiness was known to the whole town. Teresa, who desired to share the benefit of such a guidance, asked Father Baltasar to admit her among the number of his penitents, and she found in him a worthy successor to Father Juan de Padranos. The visit over, Teresa returned to the Convent of the Incarnation rejoicing in the thought that she would be free, for a time at least, to live in peace with God in her own little cell.

But the people of Avila had begun to talk about the extraordinary graces that were being showered on this nun whom they had known from girlhood. Dr. Daza was still convinced that he had been right in his judgment, and Don Francisco de Salcedo had too much confidence in his friend's learning to believe that he could have been mistaken. Both were sincerely interested in Teresa's welfare and were extremely anxious about her condition. In their distress they talked rather indiscreetly about things which, although they did not come under the seal of Confession, had been mentioned in confidence. Some people went so far even as to warn Father Baltasar Alvarez to be on his guard against his penitent.

Although in his heart of hearts the Jesuit was convinced that God alone was working in Teresa's soul, he was humble enough to think that he

might be mistaken. He had a great regard for
both Gaspar Daza and Francisco de Salcedo; it
was just possible that they might be right and
he wrong. In any case, the test was easy: humility and obedience, which are always present when
God is working in a soul, are conspicuously
absent when the work is of the devil. Father
Baltasar let it seem to Teresa that he was not
sure himself if she were not deceived by the evil
one. In any case, he told her, if she were careful not to offend God, her consolations, even if
they were the work of Satan, would not be able
to hurt her. He ordered her to pray less, to resist
with all her might her supernatural attractions,
and he deprived her for nearly three weeks of
Holy Communion.

"There was no comfort for me either in Heaven
or on earth!" cried the Saint in her anguish;
never had she suffered so cruelly. But when the
cloud was darkest the Divine voice spoke in her
soul. "Be not afraid," it said, "it is I; I will not
abandon thee; fear not."

"O my Lord, how true a Friend Thou art!"
she cried; for all was now easy to bear. As for
Father Baltasar, while more and more convinced
that he had to deal with a Saint, his direction
increased in rigor. The thought one day suggested itself to Teresa to choose another director, who would let her pray in peace, but her

Divine Master reproved her severely. "Do not flatter thyself thou art obedient," He said, "if thou art not prepared to suffer." Presently her superiors forbade her to read the spiritual books which helped her soul the most. This tried her sorely, but Our Lord consoled her. "Do not grieve, My daughter," He said; "I will give thee a living book." She soon learned what He meant.

One day while praying Teresa saw in a vision Jesus Christ at her side, after which it seemed to her that His invisible presence never left her. When she prayed He constantly appeared to her, ravishing her soul to ecstasy. It was impossible to hide what was passing; the nuns discussed it with their friends and people began to talk of exorcising the Saint to deliver her from the deceits of the devil.

About this time Father Baltasar Alvarez left Avila, recommending to Teresa during his absence another confessor, who, on his first interview with her, decided also that her visions were the work of Satan. She must make the Sign of the Cross, he told her, whenever they appeared, and repulse the evil one with a gesture of contempt and horror. Teresa herself could not doubt that it was Our Lord whom she saw and with whom she spoke; how could she bring herself to treat Him with horror and contempt? Trembling, she asked herself the question, but to her there was only one answer. Obedience was His favorite virtue; He had been obedient unto death. But when the vision came again a few days later, even as she made the Sign of the Cross and the prescribed gesture of contempt, she fell at Our Lord's feet, beseeching Him with tears to pardon her. "Thou hast done well to obey," was the answer; "I will make the truth known."

Chapter 5

PROBATION

"O my soul's Lord, who can find words to describe what Thou art to those who trust in thee?"   —*St. Teresa*

TERESA'S outward life at this time was like that of any other nun of the Incarnation. Prayer and work and the exercises of the common life succeeded each other as usual. She was more forgetful of self and thoughtful for others than anyone else in the house, but she had always been so. The visions and ecstasies with which God favored her took place during the quiet hours of prayer in her own oratory, but this state of things was not to last.

One day as the Saint knelt absorbed in God, she beheld at her side the vision of an Angel whose face shone like the sun. In his hand he held a golden dart, the point of which was all on fire, and which he plunged several times into her heart. The love of God, Teresa tells us, increased so much in her soul after this mirac-

ulous transfixion that she longed to die in order
to be no more separated from her Divine Master. Her ecstasies and visions increased, and it
became harder than ever to hide the extraordinary graces with which she was favored. Sometimes in the convent chapel before the whole
community she would be rapt in ecstasy and
raised above the ground, while the supernatural
beauty of her face struck everyone with awe.
Strange lights shone about her as she prayed,
and were seen by many.

Teresa, whose one desire was to remain hidden and unnoticed, implored of God that He
would cease to bestow on her these outward
manifestations of His favor. She sought as much
as possible the solitude of her own cell, where
no one could be witness of what passed between
her and her Divine Lord. Longing to do something for His glory, to give herself to Him as
He had given Himself to her and to satisfy the
burning love of her heart, she made, with her
director's permission, a vow to do in all things
what would be most pleasing to His Majesty.

For many years God had been preparing Teresa
for the work which He had for her to do. The
supreme test was yet to come; her soul was to
be tried as gold is tried in the fire. The lights
died out and the consolations faded away. Suffering of soul succeeded to suffering of body;

all that had passed in her hours of ecstasy seemed but the shadow of a dream. Doubts, fears and scruples assailed her. It seemed to her that she was the vilest of sinners—that, deceived herself, she was deceiving others. So did the evil one seek to drive her to despair—yet was he defeated in his attempt. For He who had been blessed in the time of joy was blessed also in the time of sorrow. Teresa clung to the thought of His mercy and praised His Holy Name.

The devil, jealous of the work of God, only redoubled his attacks. Hideous apparitions beset her, but Teresa, with the cross in her hand, defied the powers of evil. "They can do nothing without Christ's permission," she would say contemptuously. "What have we to fear?"

If the good people of Avila had been anxious before, they were much more anxious now, for rumors of what was passing travelled through the nuns of the Incarnation. Certain friends went as far as to tell Teresa that she was possessed, but she answered them with gentleness and humility: "You have only to look at the results. I was poor, and God has made me rich; everybody must see how He has changed me. Never will I believe that the devil could have given me strength to fight against my faults and to practice the opposite virtues. God has given me courage to do and bear all things for His sake. I was weak, and He has made me strong."

The truth of her words could not be denied, and God Himself was to bear testimony to it.

Although there were many Saints in Spain at that time, none was more revered than St. Peter of Alcantara, a Franciscan friar who had lived a rigorous life of prayer, fasting and penance, devoting himself entirely to the service of God and the salvation of sinners. To his eyes the veils that hide the unseen were transparent, and he could read men's souls like a book. The news reached Doña Guiomar that the holy Franciscan was engaged in a visitation of his order which would bring him to Avila, and she determined that Teresa should see him.

It was not difficult to obtain permission to take her away from the convent for a short visit, and the plan was immediately carried into execution. The two Saints understood each other at once. All Teresa's difficulties were smoothed away and her doubts completely set at rest. God and God alone was working in her, said St. Peter of Alcantara; she need have no fear.

But the holy old man was not satisfied with this. Rumors of the gossip in the town had reached his ears, and he went straight to Father Baltasar Alvarez, with whom he had a long interview and from whom he heard much of Teresa's obedience and humility. His next visit was to

Don Francisco de Salcedo, whom he succeeded in convincing of the truth, and he even managed to persuade Dr. Daza that he had been mistaken. Before leaving Avila he bade Teresa write to him whenever she wanted counsel and advice and promised to do all that he could to help her.

Consoled and strengthened, Teresa was ready now to bear the worst. The verdict of St. Peter of Alcantara was not without its effects in Avila. The gossip died down, and the nuns of the Incarnation at last began to believe that they might possibly have a Saint in their midst.

It was about this time that Teresa had a fearful vision in which God showed her the place in Hell that would have been hers had she been unfaithful to His inspirations. "All the horrors I had ever seen," cries the Saint, "were nothing compared to that; I have no words to express it. The most painful thing of all was the certainty that such torment is eternal, that there is no hope, no end to it. It only lasted a moment, but when I think of it, my blood freezes in my veins."

After the vision came the thought that souls, created like hers to know and love God, were daily falling into that place of torment. "What can I do, O my Lord, to save them?" she cried in anguish.

The answer came in a secret inspiration.

A desire took shape in Teresa's heart to lead a more mortified religious life, to keep the Rule of Mount Carmel in all its old perfection, to pray day and night as the Carmelites had prayed of old, before the Mitigated Rule had made their life so easy. She pictured to herself a convent, poor as the cave of Bethlehem, secluded, silent, full of ardent souls who lived for God's glory and who prayed for the work of holy Church and for the souls of sinners. Such was her dream—how far away it seemed!

*   *   *   *   *

It was the feast of Our Lady of Mount Carmel, and the guests that had been taking part in the festivities at the convent were dispersing to their homes. The day was drawing to a close, and Teresa was hoping for a quiet hour in her oratory when Juana Suarez, the friend of her girlhood, came to her cell for a little talk. She was soon followed by Anne and Iñez de Tapia, two cousins of Teresa's, lately professed, and two of her nieces who were being brought up at the convent—Maria and Leonora de Ocampo.

The conversation went briskly; Maria de Ocampo, a beautiful girl, whose charms were set off to the best advantage, was full of questions about the religious life. The two young nuns spoke of the Feast, and of the difficulty of preserving recollection among so many visitors.

"Very well, then," said Maria decidedly, "let all of us who are here go to some other place where we can live a solitary life like hermits; if we had courage to do that, we could found a convent." Teresa, surprised at such a suggestion from such a quarter, asked where the money was to come from. "From me," retorted Maria promptly; "I will give part of my dowry." Her sister was enchanted, the two young nuns not less so. Juana Suarez alone threw cold water on the scheme; the difficulties, she thought, would be too great. The question was discussed with all the enthusiasm of youth; plans were made and the little convent built—at least in the imagination of the company.

The next day when Doña Guiomar came to the convent, Teresa laughingly told her of the project of her young kinswomen. "It is the inspiration of God," said Doña Guiomar, "and I will help you to carry it out. Let us pray over it until we can see what to do."

For Teresa the most essential thing was to know God's will in the matter, and she earnestly prayed that He would make it clear. One morning after Holy Communion, she tells us, Our Lord appeared to her and bade her take the work to heart. The new convent was to be dedicated to St. Joseph, and Teresa was to consult Father Baltasar Alvarez and tell him what had passed. The latter suggested that she should ask the advice of Father Angel de Salasar, Provincial of the Carmelites, whereupon Doña Guiomar undertook to lay their plans before him. Meanwhile Teresa wrote to St. Peter of Alcantara, St. Francis Borgia and the Dominican St. Louis Bertrand to ask their counsel. The reply was unanimous; the three Saints blessed the project and bade Teresa accomplish it as quickly as possible. Doña Guiomar was equally successful in her embassy; the Provincial was encouraging and promised to take the new convent under his charge.

It seemed as if there was nothing left but to find a house and to found the convent; but this was not so easy. The nuns of the Incarnation, as well as the people of Avila, were quite contented with the Mitigated Rule and were highly indignant at the idea that it could be improved upon. What was the use, they asked, of going back to the Primitive Rule with all its hardships, its solitude and silence? The idea was received with ridicule. "Let Teresa keep quiet in her own convent," said the townspeople, "instead of trying to turn everything upside down; and let Doña Guiomar mind her own business and not get herself talked about."

Others said that Teresa was mad to think of leaving a convent where she was so comfortable. The storm of tongues grew apace; nuns, priests and people were against the idea. Every movement of the two friends was watched and remarked upon; the whole town was in a tumult. But Teresa was used to suffering and contradiction. On a little bookmarker that she kept in her breviary she had written the following words. They were the secret of her calm:

> "Let nothing trouble thee;
> Let nothing affright thee.
> All things pass away;
> God alone changes not;
> Patience obtains all things.
> To him who possesses God
> Nothing is wanting;
> God alone suffices."

It was necessary to seek in Avila itself a wise counselor who would give them his support. They found him in Father Pedro Ibañez, first theologian of the Convent of St. Dominic. He had been professor at the University of Salamanca and was a great student; he was, moreover, revered in Avila as a Saint. When Teresa and Doña Guiomar exposed their plans to him, he asked for a week to think it over and spent the time in prayer. Certain people of the town warned him to have nothing to do with the project, but he had sought a better Counselor. When Teresa and Doña Guiomar returned a week later, the verdict was clear and decisive. Father Pedro would give them all the help in his power, for the work was of God.

Chapter 6

THE DIVINE MISSION

"With so good a Friend and Captain ever present, Himself the first to suffer, everything can be borne. He helps, He strengthens, He never fails; He is the true Friend."   —-*St. Teresa*

THE most influential man in Avila having pronounced himself in favor of Teresa's enterprise, several others took courage to come forward to her assistance. Don Francisco de Salcedo and Gaspar Daza offered to do all in their power to help, and some of the greatest enemies of the scheme were converted. An unassuming little house on the outskirts of the town was for sale; negotiations were at once set on foot to buy it.

But things were not destined to go so smoothly. As the excitement died down in the town, it increased in the Convent of the Incarnation. Teresa's desire to found a convent of the Primitive Rule was looked upon by the nuns as a personal affront to themselves. Some even suggested that Teresa should be kept in confinement; others, but not many, took her part; the discussions grew bitter. Complaint after complaint was sent to the Provincial, who began to regret that he had ever consented to befriend the undertaking. Weary at last of the continual worry, he told Teresa that he considered himself obliged to withdraw his permission to found, urging as his reason that the opposition was too great and that the money promised was not sufficient. Teresa, undaunted, told Father Baltasar of the refusal and asked him what she should do. She was to obey, he answered, and give up all thought of the foundation.

It seemed for the moment as if Teresa's efforts and sufferings had been in vain, but her faith was great. If it was God's will that the convent should be founded, she reflected, this would certainly be done. In the meantime, her business was obedience, and she resolved to practice it as perfectly as possible. Neither in word nor in thought would she allow herself to revert to the project that had been so dear to her heart; in silence and in peace she went about her usual work at the convent. When Father Ibañez came to see her she spoke to him of God and of the spiritual life, but not one word on the subject of the foundation. It seemed as if she had completely forgotten that such an idea had ever existed, but Father Ibañez knew that this could not be so and was greatly impressed by her obedience.

Although Teresa had obeyed, her friends were under no such obligation. Doña Guiomar, at Father Ibañez' suggestion, had applied to Rome for a brief authorizing the foundation; Don Francisco and Gaspar Daza were also at work, and Teresa's docility seemed to be bringing a blessing on their endeavors.

Six months had passed when Father Ibañez suddenly resolved to leave Avila to devote himself in silence and solitude to a life of prayer. His departure seemed a serious loss to the little group of workers, but God was to provide for Teresa another friend, who was destined to take his place.

The rector of the College of St. Giles was shortly afterward withdrawn, and Father Gaspar de Salazar, a strong, wise and holy man, was put in his place. Father Baltasar Alvarez hastened to seek his advice with regard to St. Teresa, who was presently ordered to give the rector an account of her soul and of the supernatural manifestations that she had received.

This was a thing which the Saint disliked extremely, but no sooner had she entered the confessional than she was at peace. A secret intuition that Father Gaspar would understand and help her made everything easy.

Teresa was not mistaken. God had given Father Gaspar a special grace for the reading of souls. He bade the Saint's confessor give her more liberty and fear nothing; the Spirit of God was there. A little later the Saint received an order from Our Lord to speak to Father Gaspar on the subject of the new foundation. "Bid him meditate," said her Divine Master, "on the words, 'O Lord, how great are Thy works! Thy thoughts are exceeding deep.'" Father de Salazar did so, and during his prayer he saw the whole enterprise in the light of God. That very day he told Teresa that the Divine Will had been made known to him; she must go on with the undertaking.

It was agreed that they should work in secret, for the nuns of the Incarnation had prejudiced the Provincial so strongly against the project that it would have been worse than useless to appeal to him again. The state of affairs seemed anything but promising. Teresa was watched and distrusted by her sisters in religion; the required funds were not forthcoming; there was much to be done, and she alone could do it. "Ah, my beloved Master," she cried, "why do You command me to do impossible things? What can I do? What am I good for? I have neither money nor knowledge."

But there is something more necessary than

either money or knowledge to succeed in God's work, and that is holiness. At her Saviour's feet Teresa found courage to endure for her Lord's sake all the difficulties that lay before her.

Her first step was to write to her sister Juana, married to a young nobleman of Alba, Don Juan de Ovalle, to ask if her husband could come to Avila and conclude the bargain for the little house they had in view. He came at once and bought the house in his own name, taking up his abode in it with his wife, which made it possible for Teresa to visit them and so to make her plans. But the young couple was not rich, and could give little more than their good will. Part of the price at least must be paid down, and workmen would have to be hired at once to set the place in order.

Teresa as usual had recourse to prayer. As she prayed, St. Joseph appeared to her and bade her put the work in hand, for the money would be forthcoming when required. The workmen were accordingly engaged, plans made and the necessary alterations begun. A few days later the Saint received a present of a large sum of money from her brother Lorenzo in Peru. She was thus able to pay both the workmen and the creditors.

The house which they had bought was so small that it seemed impossible to turn it into

a convent, and Teresa was greatly puzzled as to
how to fit in the dormitory and recreation room,
not to mention the little chapel. While she was
trying to solve the difficulty Our Lord spoke to
her. "Have I not already told thee to go in?"
He said. "How often have I slept in the open
air because I had no roof to shelter Me."

Teresa humbled herself at her Divine Master's
feet and went back to the task with fresh courage;
this time everything seemed simple, and she saw
at once how she could manage.

The presence of the workmen made the small
house rather a comfortless dwelling for Juana
and her husband, but neither of them thought
of complaining. One day their little son Gonsalvo, aged five, was playing among the workmen's materials when part of a wall that was
being knocked down fell upon him. Crushed
and senseless, the child lay under the ruins for
several hours and was at last found by his father,
who, thinking him dead, carried him into the
house in speechless anguish and laid him on
Teresa's knees.

The Saint bent her head over the inanimate
little body, lowered her veil and prayed silently.
Presently Gonsalvo opened his eyes, smiled, sat
up and threw his little arms round his aunt's
neck. "Do not be troubled," said Teresa to her
sister, who was kneeling beside her, weeping bit-

terly. "Here is your son, take him." Both Juana and her husband believed that their child had been given back to them through Teresa's prayers.

Another strange accident showed that the evil one was doing all in his power to hinder the work. A strong wall which had just been carefully built fell suddenly during the night. "It will have to be rebuilt," said Teresa serenely when she heard the news.

"But we have not the money," objected Doña Guiomar.

"It will come," replied the Saint; and it did, that very day. Don Juan was for making the workmen rebuild the wall at their own expense, but Teresa would not hear of it. "Poor men!" she said. "It is not their fault. I know whose doing it is. What efforts Satan makes to prevent the work! But it will be carried through in spite of him." The building was indeed getting on, and the transformation of the house was nearly complete. It had been turned into the poorest little convent conceivable. Teresa's dreams seemed at last on the verge of fulfillment.

But in spite of all the care taken to preserve secrecy, suspicions had arisen as to what was going on. There was danger that these might come to the ears of the Provincial and that he would order Teresa to give up the enterprise. In that case, she would have to obey, and the work would be brought to a standstill. Our Lord, however, had His own ways of providing against this difficulty.

Although Teresa was not appreciated in her native town, rumors of her holiness had reached as far as Toledo. St. Peter of Alcantara had borne witness to her sanctity, no less than St. Francis Borgia and Father Pedro Ibañez. It began to be whispered about that there was a nun in the little town of Avila whose power of prayer was so great that God granted everything she asked of Him.

One of the greatest ladies of Toledo, Luisa, Duchess de la Cerda, had just lost her husband. It was her first great sorrow; the world which had hitherto smiled so brightly upon her seemed to be changed into a desolate wilderness. So great was her grief that her life was despaired of, when someone spoke to her of Teresa. Surely, thought the young Duchess in her anguish, a soul so beloved of God would have comfort for a sorrow such as hers. She wrote to Father Angel de Salasar, the Provincial of the Carmelites, to ask if the Saint might pay her a visit.

Teresa's surprise was great when she received an order from the Provincial to go to Toledo to be the guest of the widowed Duchess de la Cerda, who hoped for consolation from her presence. How could the Duchess have heard of her existence, she asked herself, and what would be the result if she left the work that was just about to be brought successfully to a close? She sought counsel of her Divine Master and heard in an ecstasy Our Lord speaking to her. "Go, daughter," He said; "pay no attention to those who would detain you. Fear not, I will be with you."

Father Gaspar de Salazar, hearing from Teresa of the order she had received and of Our Lord's injunctions, urged her to start at once. Confiding therefore the completion of the convent to her sister and brother-in-law, she set out for Toledo accompanied by a nun of the Convent of the Incarnation and with Don Juan de Ovalle as escort.

Chapter 7

SILENCE AND PATIENCE

"Let us somewhat resemble our King, who had no house save the stable at Bethlehem, wherein He was born, and the Cross, on which He died."   —*St. Teresa*

TERESA found Doña Luisa de la Cerda in bed, exhausted with the violence of her grief and refusing all consolation. The Saint set to work at once to comfort her both in soul and body, and after a few days succeeded in inducing her to accept the Divine Will with love and generosity.

The young Duchess resolved to spend the rest of her life in the service of God and in good works, and she felt sure that no one could teach her to do so as well as Teresa. Her new friend must stay with her, she declared, until she was strong enough to stand alone. Her love and veneration for the Saint showed itself in ways that were often more of a cross to her guest than anything else. The humble Carmelite was treated in the palace of the Duchess as if she had been a queen; everybody bowed before her and did her honor; her slightest wish was consulted.

To Teresa, whose only desire was to live in her little convent of St. Joseph in the poverty and simplicity of Bethlehem, life in a palace with its pomp and etiquette was a kind of martyrdom. But if the adulation of the members of the great household made small impression on the Saint, her holiness had much effect on them. Everyone came to seek her advice and to ask her questions. The relations and friends of Doña Luisa wanted always to be with her, for she had help and counsel for all.

Among these was a young girl, Maria de Salazar, distinguished no less for her wit than for her beauty. It was not long before Teresa's eyes had pierced through the worldly and brilliant exterior and read in Maria's heart a long-cherished wish to give herself to God in religion. "Are these quite fit," she said one day gently, touching the rich jewels which served to set off the young girl's beauty, "for one who desires to be the bride of Christ?" Maria, who had told no one of her secret, was greatly astonished; but Teresa, who saw in her an ardent and generous soul well-suited to help her in her plan of reform, did all she could to ground Maria in the principles of religious life.

It was while Teresa was at Toledo that she made the acquaintance of Mother Mary of Jesus, a Carmelite nun of Granada who, like herself, had long cherished the plan of founding a convent of the Primitive Rule. She had just returned from Rome, whither she had gone with the permission of her superiors to obtain a brief from the Pope authorizing her foundation. She had then heard of Teresa's undertaking and had set out at once for Toledo to see her. The two nuns talked long and earnestly of the project that was so dear to their hearts. Mother Mary was both holy and austere, but she had neither Teresa's breadth of mind nor her intelligence. Her work was not to prosper until it had been incorporated with that of the Saint.

From the Carmelite of Granada Teresa learned something unknown to her beforehand—that the Primitive Rule forbade the endowment of monasteries. She determined, therefore, to start her little foundation without revenues; but when her friends at Avila heard of this resolve, there was a general outcry; all were against it. It so happened that St. Peter of Alcantara, passing through Toledo at that moment, went to see Teresa, who told him all about her project and the remonstrances of her friends. The holy Franciscan was too great a lover of poverty to agree with them; he encouraged Teresa in her determination to

found without endowment. Shortly afterward,
Our Lord Himself intimated to the Saint that
it was His Will that she should do so, and those
who had been so much against it came round
in the end to the same view.

The days were long past when the constant
distractions among which she lived in Doña
Luisa's palace would have disturbed Teresa's recollection. She prayed at Toledo as she had prayed
at Avila, and her ecstasies and visions continued. Although she sought with the greatest care
to conceal these favors from those around her,
she was not always successful. People surprised
her sometimes while the divine light was still
shining from her face and her thoughts were
wholly rapt in God.

One day a servant who had long suffered from
severe pains in the head and ears begged the
Saint to make the Sign of the Cross on her fore-
head. "What are you thinking of?" cried Teresa.
"Make the Sign of the Cross yourself." But even
as she pushed the woman gently away, her hand
accidentally touched the aching head, and the
pain was instantly cured.

In the meantime, the Duchess was becoming
more and more attached to her new friend, and
it began to seem as if Teresa's stay at Toledo
might be prolonged indefinitely. The Provincial
made no step to recall her to Avila, and her

friends were losing heart. Juana had gone home to Alba, leaving her husband as guardian of the unfinished convent, and he, uncertain what to do, suddenly resolved to go to Toledo to ask Teresa's advice. It was decided that it would be better for him to go back to his wife after having made a few necessary arrangements at Avila. But no sooner had Don Juan returned to the little convent than he was suddenly seized with fever.

It was at this moment that Teresa received permission from the Provincial to return to her convent. In spite of Doña Luisa's lamentations, the Saint set out for Avila and, passing by St. Joseph's on her way, found her brother-in-law ill and in great need of assistance. Obedience obliged her to return directly to the Incarnation, but she promised to come back as soon as she could to nurse him, and she found no difficulty in obtaining permission to do so.

Teresa realized in a moment how God had blessed her enterprise during her absence. The brief had just arrived from Rome authorizing the foundation of the little Convent of St. Joseph. It was to be a house of the Primitive Rule under the jurisdiction of the diocesan Bishop of Avila, and nobody else was to interfere with its affairs.

The Saint decided that now was the moment to found. Many of her most devoted friends happened at that moment to be in Avila. St. Peter of Alcantara was the guest of Don Francisco de Salcedo; Dr. Gaspar Daza and Father Gaspar de Salazar, rector of the Jesuit College of St. Giles, were both present in the town, together with the Bishop, Monsignor Alvaro de Mendoza.

The building was pushed on to completion, while a private meeting, presided over by St. Peter of Alcantara, was held to decide what was to be the first step in the matter. It was unanimously agreed that the Bishop's approval must be sought without delay, and the case was laid before him. But when he learned that it was proposed to found the convent without endowment, he refused his sanction. St. Peter of Alcantara was ill in bed when the bad news was brought to him. Worn out with his long life of penance, his health was failing fast, and he knew that he was near his end, but his spirit was as dauntless as ever. Rising, he announced his intention of going himself to see the Bishop; and as his legs were too weak to support him, he had himself set on a mule and so made his way to the episcopal residence. To such a petitioner Monsignor de Mendoza could refuse nothing; he agreed to take the foundation under his jurisdiction and to protect it against all attacks.

Before leaving Avila, the holy Franciscan visited the convent. "This is indeed a house of Joseph, a true cave of Bethlehem," he said, delighted with its poverty.

In the meantime, the building was progressing rapidly. On the very day it was finished Don Juan's fever left him, and he understood what God had done. "It is not necessary for me to be ill any more," he said, laughing, and took lodgings in the town, that Teresa might be more at liberty to make her arrangements. The next thing was to gather the little community. The first postulants were Antonia de Henao, a connection of the Saint's proposed by St. Peter of Alcantara; Maria de Paz, an adopted child of Doña Guiomar's; Ursula de Revilla, a penitent of Dr. Daza's; and Maria, a sister of Father Julian of Avila, a young priest who was to be the chaplain of the little convent.

On the Feast of St. Bartholomew these first foundation stones of the Reformed Carmelites arrived at St. Joseph's and were welcomed by Teresa, who at once led them to the chapel. There, in the presence of the few faithful friends who had championed the undertaking, Mass was said by Dr. Daza, the Bishop's delegate, and the Blessed Sacrament placed in the Tabernacle. The rough habits of the Reform were then blessed, the postulants were clothed, the *Te Deum* was chanted and the dream of Teresa's life was accom-

plished. Prostrate before the altar, the newly made
novices poured out their hearts in love and grat-
itude to God, while the Saint, rapt in ecstasy,
seemed to be already in Heaven.

Teresa had long ago determined that in order
to efface all differences of rank in the nuns of
the Reformed Carmel they should take symbolic
names borrowed from the Saints and Angels or
from the mysteries of Our Lord's life. Antonia
de Henao therefore became Antonia of the Holy
Ghost; Ursula de Revilla, Ursula of the Saints;
Maria de Paz, Maria of the Cross; and Father
Julian's sister, Maria of St. Joseph. To Teresa's
great regret she could not herself assume the
rough habit and coarse sandals prescribed by the
Primitive Rule, for she was still personally under
the jurisdiction of the Provincial. Even her permission to remain at St. Joseph's might be any
day withdrawn, granted, as it had been, that she
might nurse her brother-in-law, who was now
strong and well.

Father Daza and his friends had left, the cer-
emony was long over, but Teresa could not tear
herself away from the Tabernacle. The little convent was at last founded; the Rule of Carmel
was at last to be practiced in all its perfection;
that which God had commanded had been done.
The evil one, beaten at every point, was to make
one last attempt on the chosen soul who had

been appointed to carry out God's plans. Teresa was suddenly assailed with anguish as Satan suggested to her that she had made the foundation without her superior's consent. The commands of Our Lord Himself, the counsel of His Saints, the sanction of her director, the brief from Rome—all were forgotten. Doubts and fears overwhelmed her. How would these delicately nurtured young girls be able to stand the austerities of the Primitive Rule? How would the convent be provided for, founded as it was without endowment? How could she herself, weak in health, bear the new life in all its strictness? So did the tempter seek to drive her to despair; but Teresa called on her Divine Master, and the clouds at last began to break. Had she not asked Our Lord to let her suffer for His sake? What then was to be feared?

Summoning all her courage, Teresa promised before the Tabernacle that she would not rest until she had obtained permission from her superiors to live entirely at St. Joseph's. As she made the promise, the temptation left her.

Chapter 8

ST. JOSEPH'S

"A cowardly soul, afraid of anything but sin against God, is a very unseemly thing, when we have on our side the King omnipotent."
—*St. Teresa*

THE news that the Convent of St. Joseph had been actually founded spread through Avila like wildfire. The poorer people in their simple faith hailed it with joy, but those who from the first had been against it gave full vent to their indignation and did all in their power to influence the public against it. This unendowed convent, they cried, would take the bread out of the mouths of the poor; it was a novelty, moreover, and the interests of the town demanded that it should be suppressed at once. "If the Moors had invaded Avila," said Father Julian, "and set the whole town on fire, the disturbance could scarcely have been greater."

When the news reached the Convent of the Incarnation, Teresa was severely blamed. She was insulting the whole Order, cried the nuns, by attempting to lead a more perfect life than its other members, and the Prioress was induced to order her instant return to the Incarnation.

It was hard to leave the young novices alone, but Teresa's first thought was obedience. Having blessed and embraced her little family, she commended it to Our Lord and St. Joseph, placed Ursula of the Saints in charge of the small household, and departed. No sooner had she arrived at the Incarnation than she was summoned before the Prioress and the elder members of the community to explain her conduct. She gently answered all the questions put to her, excused herself in no way for what she had done, and asked pardon if she had been in any way to blame.

It was then decided that she should be questioned by the Provincial, and Father Angel de Salasar was hastily summoned. Before the assembled nuns he rebuked Teresa sharply for her action, but not a word in her own defense passed her lips. Standing before them all like a culprit, she humbly listened to what Father de Salasar had to say, begging only that she might be punished and then forgiven.

The Provincial, touched by Teresa's humility, counseled indulgence, but of this the nuns would not hear. Her doings were a source of scandal to the town, they declared; she was the most imperfect among them all and had only founded the monastery that people might think well of her. To these accusations Teresa only replied that it was perfectly true, that she was the greatest sinner in the convent.

Father de Salasar was thoroughly perplexed; turning at last to Teresa, he bade her declare before the assembled company the reasons that had moved her to act as she had done. The simple eloquence of her reply impressed him so much that, dismissing the nuns, he ordered her to speak to him fully of all that had passed between her Divine Master and herself, the counsel she had taken and the means she had employed.

Father de Salasar was an upright man and a good religious. As he listened to Teresa's humble recital and realized how careful she had been not to act in any way against obedience, he was now as much in her favor as he had been against her. Dismissing her at last with his blessing, he promised to allow her to return to St. Joseph's as soon as the turmoil had subsided.

There was no sign of this, however. A meeting was held in the town hall by the people of Avila at which it was decided that the new convent should be suppressed and the novices sent back to their homes. When told of this decision the little community flatly refused to obey; they appealed to their God and to the King. They were under the jurisdiction of the Bishop alone, they said, and he alone could dismiss them.

The Governor, undaunted, held another meeting, at which it was declared that the convent had been founded without the consent of the town and was on this account illegal. The Blessed Sacrament must therefore be removed, the nuns expelled and the house pulled down. The order was about to be given when a learned Dominican, Father Bañez, rose to his feet and addressed the people. Teresa de Ahumada, he explained, was unknown to him except by name; he had never even seen her; he was therefore wholly unbiased in the matter.

"But it is a marvel to me," he continued, "that the townspeople of Avila can believe that a few poor women hidden in their cells should constitute a danger to the public or be a burden on the town. What is the reason for this meeting? Is there an enemy at our gates? Is the town on fire? Are plague and famine among us? No. Four humble Carmelites are praying in an obscure quarter of the city. Moreover, the Bishop alone has power to deal with the question, for the Holy See has placed the convent under his jurisdiction. Let those who think the foundation illegal make their complaints to him."

Father Bañez was a man of weight in Avila; his opinion was respected, and for the moment the danger was averted. The Governor was obliged to give way, and the meeting was dispersed; but the Saint's enemies were determined not to be beaten. They did all in their power to induce the Provincial and the Prioress of the Incarnation to compel Teresa to submit to their will, and the storm raged on without abating.

The Saint's friends were not idle either. Father Julian of Avila, who had constituted himself Teresa's devoted squire and chaplain, went backward and forward between St. Joseph's and the Convent of the Incarnation bringing Teresa news of her daughters and returning with words of comfort and consolation to the orphaned community. Father Gaspar Daza was also watching over the new foundation, zealously training the novices in the ways of the spiritual life, while Don Francisco de Salcedo provided for their temporal necessities.

The authorities of Avila finally decided to lay the case before the King's Council. Many of Teresa's friends interested themselves in her cause, and the lawsuit ended in a complete triumph for the Reform, the Council blaming the Governor severely for his action in the matter. It only remained for Teresa to obtain permission to return to St. Joseph's, but this the Provincial hesitated to grant. Father Pedro Ibañez, who had befriended the Saint at the beginning of her enterprise and who was back for a short time in Avila, did all in his power on her behalf. Even the Bishop, Don Alvaro de Mendoza, wrote to Father Angel de Salasar, but with no effect. Teresa at last took the matter into her own hands. "Beware, my Father, of resisting the Holy Ghost," she said one day solemnly to the Provincial. At her words his hesitation vanished. He not only gave her permission herself to return to St. Joseph's, but even allowed her to take with her some nuns from the Incarnation who wished to join the Reform.

Who shall describe the joy at the little convent as Teresa crossed the threshold! Her first visit was to the chapel to thank God for all His mercies and to offer herself and her little flock to Him forever. There at the foot of the Tabernacle she saw in a vision her Lord, who, stooping lovingly toward her, placed a crown on her head and blessed her for what she had done in His service. Then the Saint, together with her companions from the Incarnation, put on the coarse habit and the rough sandals of the Reform. Doña Teresa de Ahumada was now Teresa of Jesus.

And what of the little convent that she had founded? Father Julian of Avila, who wrote the history of the foundation forty-two years later, says:

"God willed to have a house in which He could recreate Himself; a house in which He could take up His abode; a garden in which flowers should grow not of the kind which bloom on earth, but those which bloom only in Heaven."

It was truly the little sanctuary of which Teresa had dreamed, a place of prayer and penance for the salvation of souls where God was served in perfect fidelity.

The thought of the end for which the convent had been founded was ever present to the Saint. "Let us help by our prayers," she would say to her novices, "the apostolic men who are working in the world to save sinners, for they are the servants of our King. If we contribute to their success by our prayers we shall also have fought, we in our solitude, for God's cause."

Mortification, obedience and humility were the virtues Teresa required of her daughters, together with a holy joy and freedom of heart in God's service. The different duties of the little household were divided among its members, Teresa taking her turn in the kitchen with the others and working harder than them all. It was remarked that when it was her turn to cook, everything that she needed seemed to come as if by magic. It was as if Our Lord, knowing how she delighted in making a little feast for her daughters, took care to provide the means.

On other days, when the fare was scanty, she would so speak to them of the love of God that their hearts were all on fire and every privation was forgotten. When the nuns were not at prayer or chanting the Divine Office, they spent their time in spinning or mending; every moment was turned to account, for idleness, as Teresa well knew, opens a door to many evils. The recreations, presided over by the Saint, were full of gaiety and holy joy. Teresa could not bear melancholy. "A sad nun is a bad nun," she would often say, and a depressing or depressed postulant had small chance of admittance at St. Joseph's.

No one knew better than she the weakness of human nature and the dangers of giving way to fussiness about health. She had learned by her own experience that God blesses courage in this respect, and she advised her daughters to practice it. When they were really ill, she bade them say so simply; but as for trifling ailments, it was best to think as little about them as possible. "I beg of you, my children, to bear your little ills in silence," she would say to her novices; "they are sometimes only the effect of the imagination. The more we give in the worse we get." In the time of real suffering they were to lift up their thoughts to Heaven. "How sweet it will

be for us at the hour of death," she cries, "to
go to be judged by Him whom we have loved
above all things! . . . What happiness to think
we are not going to a strange country, but to
our own, since it is the home of that beloved
Spouse whom we love so much, and by whom
we are so much loved!"

The Bishop of Avila, Don Alvaro de Mendoza, visited the convent frequently and was
delighted with the fervor of the nuns. One day
he brought with him a beautiful crucifix, which
Teresa begged leave to show to the community.
She had returned to the parlor and was talking
to the Bishop when the sound of voices singing
led her to open the door leading into the cloister. A little procession had been formed by the
novices, at the head of which marched the
youngest postulant holding the crucifix aloft and
singing the litany of the Holy Name. Instead,
however, of "Have mercy on us," they were chanting fervently, "Stay with us." The application
was obvious, and Teresa was a little ashamed of
her daughters, but the Bishop only laughed.
Needless to say, the crucifix remained at St.
Joseph's.

In the autumn of 1566 a holy missionary,
Father Maldonado, came to see Teresa. He had
just returned from the West Indies and had sad
tales to tell of the ignorance and vice of the

natives. For some days after his departure the Saint could do nothing but pray to God to help these poor souls, that they might not be lost eternally. As she knelt weeping before the Tabernacle Our Lord appeared and said to her, "Wait a little while, My daughter, and great things shall be revealed to you."

Six months later the Saint heard that Father John Baptist Rubeo, General of the Order of Mount Carmel, was on his way to Spain to visit the houses of his order. She was not without fear that the General might disapprove of her reform and use his authority to order her to return to the Incarnation; so, bidding her daughters pray, she sent him a humble invitation to visit St. Joseph's.

Now the General, who was a wise and holy man, had come to Spain at the request of the King with the intention of introducing certain reforms among the Spanish Carmelites. At St. Joseph's he found all he had dreamed of and more—the very spirit of Carmel in all its ancient integrity. It was the desire of his heart, he said to Teresa, that such a seed should take root and spread; it was the very realization of all his hopes. Among the houses of the Mitigated Rule he found little zeal for reform and he returned frequently during the time of his stay in Spain to talk over difficulties and discuss plans with the

Saint. His wish was that she should found other convents of the Primitive Rule, holding their authority straight from the Generals of the Order, and this he gave her leave to do in any places in the province of Castile where the Ordinary of the diocese would give permission.

Don Alvaro de Mendoza, the Bishop, was very anxious to found houses of the Primitive Rule for men also, but here the General hesitated. The time, he said, was not quite ripe for such an undertaking; it would come later. He had already set out on his return journey to Rome when he received a message from Teresa earnestly begging that he would grant the Bishop's request. To her he could refuse nothing. Permission was therefore given to found two monasteries of the Primitive Rule for men, on the condition that the Provincial give his consent.

Chapter 9

FOUNDATIONS

"For my part, I think that the measure of being able to bear much or little is that of love."

—*St. Teresa*

THE time had come when Teresa was to leave the sweet solitude of St. Joseph's, the life of prayer and silence that she loved so much. The work of the foundations lay before her with its long journeys, its weary correspondence, its complicated business affairs, its trials and its troubles. There is a belief abroad in the world that a life of prayer and contemplation tends to make people vague and impractical: the last ten years of St. Teresa's life are a standing proof to the contrary. Hers was a wisdom, an insight and a power wholly unknown to those who live only in the world of matter; in everything she undertook she succeeded.

About twenty miles distant from Avila lay the little town of Medina del Campo, chosen by Teresa for many reasons as the site of her second foundation. The Jesuits were already established there, and their rector, Father Baltasar Alvarez, Teresa's old friend, had promised to support the undertaking. The Prior of the Carmelites of the Mitigated Rule, Father Antonio de Heredia, was also strongly in their favor and had promised to find them a house. The one that he bought, however, was in such ill repair that it was impossible to go into it; Father Julian of Avila was therefore sent to Medina to rent a lodging in which the nuns could live until it was ready.

In the middle of August Teresa set out, accompanied by her niece Maria de Ocampo, now Sister Maria Bautista, and Sister Anne of the Angels, both from the Convent of St. Joseph's, and four nuns of the Incarnation who wished to join the Reform. They were halfway on their journey and close to the little town of Arévalo, where they were to spend the night, when they were met by a messenger from Father Julian. The proprietor of the little house he had rented, which was close to the Augustinian Convent in Medina, declared that the Augustinians objected to the Carmelites as neighbors and that he could not hold to his bargain.

Here was indeed a calamity. What was to be done? To return to Avila, they all decided, was out of the question. While her daughters slept,

Teresa prayed, and in the morning came the solution. Father Antonio de Heredia, who, eager to welcome the Saint, had come to Arévalo to escort her on her way, suggested that they should go directly to the house which he had bought. It was out of repair, it is true, but not too far gone to afford them shelter. They could call on the way at his own monastery of St. Anne's for all they required for the chapel; Mass could then be said and the convent founded at once.

The plan sounded possible, so the little company set out for Medina. It was near midnight when they reached St. Anne's, stopped to gather the furniture for the chapel and, reinforced by two of Father Antonio's friars, set off again on foot through the town, looking, as Father Julian merrily remarked, exactly like a caravan of gypsies who had robbed a church. Luckily, they met few people and proceeded unnoticed until they reached a tumbled-down old house facing the street. This was their future convent. Father Antonio must have been suffering from temporary blindness, thought St. Teresa, when he had judged it fit for habitation. Nevertheless, there they were, and the chapel had to be gotten ready.

Father Antonio and the two friars set to work with a will. The rubbish was cleared out, the place swept, hangings fixed; everybody did their best, and by daybreak all was ready. A tiny bell rang for the first Mass, and the people, greatly astonished to find that a new convent had been founded during the night, came flocking into the little chapel. The nuns assisted from behind the staircase door, for there was no grille and the place was crowded. Teresa's soul was flooded with joy at the thought that her Divine Master had another sanctuary on earth, and all trials were forgotten.

But when the Mass was over and their new abode appeared in the searching light of day, the Saint saw what the darkness of the night had mercifully hidden. The chapel was on the street, and seeing the state of dilapidation of the whole building, anyone might have gotten in; the house seemed to be tottering to its ruin. But the sight of the poverty of the new foundation only served to increase the devotion of the people, who continued to flock to the little chapel to pray. Teresa set men to watch by night, for fear of thieves, and she herself watched, lest the men should sleep. A week later a rich merchant of Medina kindly offered the upper floor of his house to the nuns while the necessary repairs were carried out.

Father Antonio de Heredia, the Prior of St. Anne's, continued to befriend the convent, and when Teresa mentioned her intention of founding a house of the Primitive Rule for men, imme-

diately offered himself as her first subject. A few
days later the Saint received a visit from a holy
old friar who had also heard of the project. He
came to recommend to her notice a young religious who, not content with the Mitigated Rule,
had resolved to join the Carthusians. The next
day, Father John of St. Matthias, as the young
friar was called, made his appearance in person.
Teresa was delighted with him; his modesty, wisdom and piety, added to his diminutive stature,
gave him something of the air of an angelic
child. "I had a friar and a half," Teresa would
say, laughing, when she told the story in later
years, "wherewith to start the Reform." But the
"half-friar," known to history as St. John of the
Cross, was to be the very prop and stay of the
whole undertaking. The Saint bade him continue his theological studies for a year until the
time should be ripe for the foundation.

In the meantime, Don Bernardino de Mendoza, younger brother of the Bishop of Avila,
had offered Teresa a house and garden if she
would found a convent at Valladolid. Scarcely
had she accepted his offer when her old friend
Doña Luisa de la Cerda came to Medina to beg
the Saint to make a foundation on her property
at Malagon. This Teresa did not see her way to
doing, so she declined. She then set out for
Alcala, whither she had been entreated to go by

a lady of the Court of Philip II who had helped Mother Mary of Jesus to found there her new Convent of the Reform. The foundation was not prospering owing to the excessive austerities of the foundress, who wrote herself begging Teresa to come and teach her the true spirit of the Order.

Such a humble plea could not be refused. The Master's interests were at stake; the Saint set out at once. Mother Mary received Teresa as an angel sent from Heaven, gave her full authority and begged her to explain how she had succeeded so wonderfully in producing the perfect life they had dreamed of together when she herself had failed.

Teresa's teaching was eagerly listened to; the austerities were diminished; the spirit of love and joy entered into the hearts of the community, and when their visitor left them two months later, all were happy and contented.

Doña Luisa was still begging for her foundation at Malagon, and induced thereto by Father Bañez' advice, Teresa decided to grant her wish. Having set all in order at Medina, she went to Toledo, taking with her four nuns from Avila. Here they were joined by an old friend, Maria de Salazar, who was the first religious to be professed at the new convent. Having remained two months at Malagon to put all in order, Teresa resolved to go to Valladolid.

But Valladolid was sixty miles away, and, worn out with hard work and travelling, the Saint fell sick at Toledo, where she was obliged to remain for rest and treatment. She was scarcely well when she set forth again, only to be attacked once more at Avila by an illness which obliged her to stay at St. Joseph's for another month, to the great delight of her daughters. While she was there, a Spanish gentleman, having heard that she proposed to found a monastery of bare-footed or "Discalced" Carmelite friars, offered her a tiny house at Durvelo, a little village near Medina. Teresa gratefully accepted the gift and visited her new property on the way to Val-ladolid. It was indeed very small, and exceed-ingly dirty; Father Julian declared that nothing could ever make it fit for a monastery, but Teresa thought otherwise and described it to Father John and Father Antonio when they came to see her at Medina. They were ready, they declared, for the love of God, to take up their abode in a stable: the sooner the better.

But Father Antonio had first to resign his office of Prior and put things in order at St. Anne's, and it was decided that while he did so, Father John of the Cross should go to Valladolid with Teresa to be instructed in the Rule of the Reform. The foundation in that town was successfully carried through, but for Durvelo the consent of the Provincial was necessary, and Teresa had not much to hope for from Father Angel de Salasar. Consent was, however, obtained by means of an influential friend, and Father John of the Cross, armed with Teresa's blessing and the coarse habit that she had made for him with her own hands, set out accompanied by a carpenter, who was to make the necessary alterations in the tiny building.

Father Antonio arrived soon after with a brother from St. Anne's, and when Teresa visited them three months later, she found the foundation in full swing. The cells, it is true, were so narrow that no one could turn around in them; the beds were of straw, with a stone for a pillow; the whole furniture consisted of a skull as a reminder of death and two sticks in the form of a cross; but the fervor of the three Fathers made up for everything.

The Primitive Rule was now planted in the heart of the Order of Carmel. There were troubles and sorrows ahead, but the grain of mustard seed had been sown; it was growing rapidly, and in time to come its branches were to reach to the ends of the earth.

Chapter 10

PRIORESS OF THE INCARNATION

> "The love and fear of God are like two
> strong castles, from which war is made against
> the world and the devil."   —*St. Teresa*

FOUNDATIONS followed each other rapidly at Toledo, Salamanca, Alba and Pastraña, in which last-named place Teresa, to her great joy, was also able to establish a second monastery of friars. She was looking forward to a time of well-earned repose with her daughters at Salamanca when the Provincial of the Mitigated Rule began to interfere with her convent at Medina. It was not the first time that this had happened, and Teresa wrote him a firm but respectful letter reminding him that all the foundations of the Reform were under the jurisdiction of the General of the Order alone. The reply of the Provincial was to cancel the election of the Prioress who had just been appointed at Medina and to put a nun of the Mitigated Rule from the Convent of the Incarnation in her place.

Teresa, who had hastened to the assistance of her daughters, was ordered, together with the deposed Prioress, to return at once to Avila under pain of severe censure. Although the convents of the Reform were not under the Provincial's jurisdiction, Teresa considered that she herself was, for she had entered and made her profession in a house of the Mitigated Rule. She therefore obeyed, although her heart was heavy at the thought of leaving her daughters at Medina in the hands of an entirely incapable superior.

It was at this very moment that, a second visitation of the Order having been arranged by Pope Pius V and Philip II, two holy and learned Dominicans were dispatched to Spain on this mission. The first stop of Father Hernandez, who had been appointed Visitor of Castile, was at the Monastery of the Barefooted Friars at Pastraña. Delighted with the fervor and austerity which he found there, he next visited the convent of nuns, the holiness of whose lives gave him an ardent desire to know the Saint who had planned and executed the Reform. Teresa was at Avila, they told him, and thither he went to see her. While there, having heard of the doings at Medina and that the intruded Prioress was heartily sick of her position, Father Hernandez determined to remedy the evil. Going straight to Medina he presided, by virtue of the authority given him by the Holy See, at a new election, at which, upon his suggestion, Teresa herself was chosen Prioress.

It took the Saint two months to repair the mischief that had been done, but peace and order were soon restored and sorrow gave way to joy. For Teresa herself, another and a heavier cross was in store, an unexpected and overwhelming sorrow. She received a letter from Father Hernandez bidding her return at once to Avila. In virtue of the authority given him over the whole Order, he had appointed her Prioress of the Convent of the Incarnation.

The task of the Visitor was certainly not an easy one. His mission was to introduce certain reforms among the Carmelites of the Mitigated Rule; to make them practice at least what their Rule enjoined. The effect produced on Father Hernandez, fresh from the convents of the Primitive Rule, by the sight of the disorder and relaxation which reigned at the Convent of the Incarnation can well be imagined. Things had not improved since Teresa's departure, and there was much need of reform in every way. How could such a state of things be remedied? Who could be found strong enough, patient and gentle enough, to introduce the necessary reforms and make these poor souls practice even the Mitigated Rule with fidelity? One person and one only seemed to him to fulfill the required conditions, and that one was Teresa.

If the appointment was a blow to Teresa, it was no less of a shock to the nuns of the Incarnation, and they resolved to resist it with all their power. Teresa would try to enforce upon them the austerities of the Primitive Rule, they protested angrily to one another. They did not want to be reformed; they were quite contented as they were. They would die, they declared, before they accepted her as Prioress.

To Teresa the burden seemed almost greater than she could bear. How could she leave her newly founded convents? Would not such a charge absorb all her time and all her strength? How could she make these nuns, already strongly prejudiced against her, practice their Rule and give up the customs to which they held so strongly? At Our Lord's feet she poured out all her misgivings and all her sorrow, and there, as always, she found the help she needed. "Take courage," said her Divine Master, "and know that it is My wish. It will not be so difficult as you think, and your foundations will not suffer. Cease to resist, for My power is great."

Early in October Teresa set out for the Convent of the Incarnation accompanied by the Provincial, Father Angel de Salasar, and another ecclesiastic. Standing in the presence of the community and the Provincial, she could not but remember another occasion when she had stood, not as now in the place of honor, but as a culprit before her judges. And yet she had suffered less then than she was suffering now.

When the act of election which made Teresa Prioress was read, the storm broke loose. Shouts and cries of indignation drowned the voice of the Provincial. A few of the nuns, who were in Teresa's favor, tried to intone the *Te Deum* and to force their way through the crowd to conduct her to the choir, but the attempt was hopeless. The Provincial threatened the rebellious party with the censures of the Church; nobody listened, and the uproar continued. Through the raging crowd Teresa at last succeeded in escaping to the chapel, where she prayed earnestly for help from Heaven. Then, returning to the chapter-room, where Father Angel was still struggling to enforce silence and submission, she went about to each nun in turn, speaking gently to each and saying aloud before them all that it was not astonishing that they should accept ungraciously a Prioress who was so unworthy of the office.

Though Teresa was at last installed, the nuns were not vanquished. When the first chapter was held, they agreed that they would declare openly that they would never recognize her as Prioress. But while they were planning, Teresa was plan-

ning too. When the nuns entered the chapter-
room, the Prioress's stall was occupied by a large
statue of Our Lady; the keys of office were in
her hand, and Teresa sat on a low stool at her
feet. The application was easy to see: Our Lady
was Prioress of the Incarnation, the Saint was
to be her humble servant; the hearts of the nuns
were softened a little, and still more so when
Teresa spoke.

"If the sacrifice of my life or of my blood
would help you," said their new Prioress, "I
would make it. Why should you look upon me
as a stranger? I am a daughter of this house and
your Reverences' sister. You need not fear my
rule. Though I have lived among the Carmelites
of the Primitive Rule, I know, by the grace of
God, how to govern those who are not of the
Reform. My wish is that we should serve God
in meekness, doing the small amount our Rule
demands out of love for Him who loves us so
much. Our Lord is merciful, and though our
weakness is great, He will help us."

The nuns' hearts were touched, and they
promised obedience to Teresa, begging her to
reform whatever was opposed to the practice of
their Rule. The first thing to be done was to
make them happy in their religious life, and to
this Teresa brought all her genius, her tact and
her knowledge of human nature. She succeeded

beyond all expectation. Gradually the visits in the parlor were diminished; Divine Office was regularly sung; cheerful recreations, spiritual reading, prayer and work took the place of the old idleness and distractions. Discontent and weariness gave way to joy and fervor.

This was not all done in a day, but by degrees, the nuns learning ever more and more to appreciate and love the Mother that God had sent them. She could read every heart and had help and sympathy for every difficulty. Full of courage herself, she had the gift of giving courage to others. When, through her influence, Father John of the Cross had been appointed confessor to the convent, Teresa could truly say that her daughters of the Incarnation bade fair to rival their sisters of the Reform in their zeal and fervor in God's service. The work that had been done, and the earnest efforts that had been made, were shortly to receive the seal of God's approval.

The nuns were all assembled on the feast day of St. Sebastian in the oratory where the first chapter had been held. They had just begun to sing the *Salve Regina* when Teresa, looking upward, saw suddenly that the statue of the Mother of God which had remained in the Prioress's stall had vanished. In place of it there stood our Blessed Lady herself, surrounded by Angels who hovered in a circle above the stalls of the community. The vision lasted until the antiphon was ended, when the nuns, struck by the sight of Teresa's radiant face, asked her eagerly what had happened and heard from her own lips the account of what she had seen.

To this day the Prioress' stall in the Convent of the Incarnation remains vacant in Our Lady's honor. The nuns sit on the footstools below their stalls, which remain also empty and are decorated with flowers in remembrance of the vision.

Chapter 11

THE LAST TRIAL

"Though trials or persecutions increase, yet
if we bear them without offending Our Lord,
rejoicing in suffering for His sake, it will be
all the greater gain."   —*St. Teresa*

TERESA had been at the Convent of the
Incarnation about two years when Father
Hernandez gave her leave to visit some of the
houses of the Reform where her presence was
urgently needed. The foundation at Pastraña especially was in a very difficult situation, for its
foundress, the Princess of Eboli, having suddenly
lost her husband, had announced her intention
of entering the convent as a nun.

The Prioress was aghast, and not without reason, for she had had some experience of the
noble lady's whims and caprices. The news that
the Princess had had herself clothed with the
habit in her own palace and was on her way to
the convent filled all hearts with a consterna-
tion which her actions only served to augment.

Her request that two of her ladies-in-waiting should be instantly admitted as novices having been refused, she sent for a Prior of the Mitigated Rule to enforce her commands. When the Prioress objected that it was altogether against the rules that she should receive in the cloisters the people who came to condole with her on her husband's death, the self-made novice replied that the convent belonged to her and she would do what she chose in it. After three weeks of religious life she departed as suddenly as she had come, dimly conscious of the fact that she had made a fool of herself and furiously indignant with everybody and everything. To satisfy her ill humor, she withdrew all that she herself as well as her husband had given to the convent, leaving the nuns in the most abject poverty.

Teresa was busy with a foundation at Segovia, but as soon as she was free she set out for Pastraña, determined to withdraw the nuns from their impossible position and to give up the house altogether. But the Princess, although she would do nothing more for the foundation, was determined that it should remain, and the community had to escape from the convent in the darkness of the night. They made their way with some difficulty to Segovia, where the Prioress was placed in charge of the new foundation.

Teresa's term of office at the Incarnation had

now expired, and she had great difficulty in preventing the nuns from re-electing her. "I love the house as my mother, and you all as my sisters," she said to them, "but I cannot remain with you. My other houses need me too much." She was then begged to choose her successor, and having named the sub-Prioress, who was immediately elected, the Saint gave herself up once more to the work of the foundations.

She was now over sixty years of age, worn out with hard work and ill health, but her spirit was as valiant as ever. "To suffer or to die" had been her constant prayer, and her longing to share in the Passion of her Divine Lord was to be satisfied more fully than ever during the last years of her life.

The Carmelite friars were not, as were their sisters of the Reform, under the direct jurisdiction of the General of the Order, but were governed by the Provincials of the Mitigated Rule. That sooner or later there would be trouble on account of this arrangement had always been foreseen by St. Teresa, but for the moment it was impossible to remedy it. The Dominican Visitors, Father Hernandez and Father Vargas, had been so delighted with the fervor and zeal of the friars of the Reform that they had established them in several new foundations, Father Vargas going so far even as to delegate to Father

Jerome Gratian, one of the most gifted among them, his own powers as Visitor of the Order.

The Carmelites of the Mitigated Rule were already jealous of the growth and prosperity of the Reform; no sooner did they hear of this new mark of favor than, filled with indignation, they denounced Father Vargas' action to their General in Rome. This new growth, they complained, was troubling the peace of the Order; there would soon be a schism in its midst. Every kind of charge was brought against the friars of the Primitive Rule. They were rebellious, disobedient; they founded new monasteries without permission; they wanted to enforce their reforms on the whole Order.

Father Rubeo believed these reports. He passed severe censures on the Barefooted friars and sent Father Tostado, a Portuguese Carmelite, to Spain to act as his representative, giving him authority to settle all the affairs of the Order. A long and weary struggle ensued. The Papal Nuncio and the King upheld the friars of the Reform, while the far more powerful body of the Mitigated Rule, with Father Tostado at their head, was determined to drive them out of their houses. Teresa prayed and suffered. The work of long years seemed in danger of being overthrown, but her trust was in God, by whose inspiration she had acted.

In the meantime, new foundations for nuns were made at Veas and Seville. The Saint started for the latter town, accompanied by a few of her daughters, in the midst of the heat of a Castilian summer. They travelled in a covered cart, and Teresa was attacked by fever on the way. The only shelter they could get was an attic directly under the roof of a poor little inn. It had no windows, and the pitiless sun beat in through the door whenever it was opened; it was easier to continue the journey than to seek rest in such a place. While they were crossing the Guadalquivir the ferryboat got adrift and they were nearly drowned.

The party was resting in a field near Alvino when a violent quarrel broke out between some peasants and soldiers who were passing. Knives and swords were drawn, things looked danger-ous and the nuns were very much alarmed. But Teresa, going straight into the midst of the com-batants, bade them remember that they were under the eyes of God, who would one day judge them. There was something in the face and voice of the Saint that strangely calmed their passion. Swords and knives were sheathed, anger was for-gotten and they went their way in peace.

At last Teresa and her daughters reached their journey's end. The convent at Seville was founded, but fresh sorrow was in store.

At the time of the foundation of Pastraña, the Princess of Eboli, having heard that the Saint, in obedience to an order of her confessor, had written an account of her life, requested that it should be given her to read. Teresa had refused, whereupon the Princess, highly indignant, represented that the privilege had been granted to the Duchess of Alba and Doña Luisa de la Cerda. Why, therefore, should she, equally a patroness of the Order, be excluded? The Saint had been obliged to yield reluctantly, but her fears were justified, for the Princess, utterly incapable of understanding what she read, had loaned the book to her friends, and Teresa was unable to recover it. Later came the death of the Prince and the unpleasant episode at Pastraña which made the Princess Teresa's inveterate enemy. Here was a chance for revenge. The great lady denounced the book to the Inquisition as unorthodox.

In spite of the fact that it had been approved by eminent theologians, Teresa herself in her humility believed that what she had written must be full of faults. She was in the greatest distress, for she feared that if the book were condemned, the scandal would fall upon the whole Order. Her apprehensions, however, were soon set at rest. The book was not only approved by the Holy Office, but commended; the spite of the

Princess had done the Saint more good than harm.

In the meantime, the affairs of the Barefooted friars were going from bad to worse. Teresa herself, as their foundress, was included in the calumnies which were daily being circulated against them. A decree of the General Chapter condemned her, in punishment for her disobedience, to confine herself to one of her convents and to remain there permanently. The Saint replied in a spirit of filial obedience, but with the deepest sorrow. Her only comfort, she wrote to Father Rubeo, in the trials she had had to bear was the consideration that she had believed herself to be carrying out his orders and doing God's will.

The nuns of Seville, before Teresa left them—forever, as they thought—obtained permission for Brother John de la Miseria, a friar of the Reform, to paint her portrait. Brother John was an unskillful artist and better at prayer than at painting; but after an incalculable number of sittings he declared that the picture was finished. "God forgive you, Brother John, for making me so ugly!" cried Teresa merrily when she saw it, "after all you have made me suffer."

In the autumn of 1576 the Saint arrived at Toledo accompanied by a young and holy lay sister, Anne of St. Bartholomew, who was henceforth to be her inseparable companion.

Father Tostado, determined to uphold the honor of the Mitigated Rule, had in the meantime called together a Provincial Chapter where it was decreed that the friars of the Reform were to be shod, to wear the usual habit and to be under the direction of the superiors of the Mitigated Rule. They were to open their houses to all who should be sent to them and go themselves, if required, to live in any house of the Order.

The decree meant the complete annihilation of the Reform. The Barefooted friars resolved to resist it to the utmost, and the friars of the Mitigated Rule resorted to violence. Father John of the Cross was imprisoned and so harshly treated that his life was in danger. Misrepresentations were sent to Rome with the result that another decree was issued, making the nuns as well as the friars of the Reform subject to the government of the superiors of the Mitigated Rule and forbidding them to receive novices. It was ruin, total and complete. When the news reached Teresa at St. Joseph's, for once her strong spirit failed her. All day long she remained alone praying and weeping in the bitterness of her heart.

It was the Eve of the Nativity, and as the night wore on, Sister Anne of St. Bartholomew knocked softly at the Saint's door and begged her to take some nourishment before she went to the choir for Matins. Having succeeded in inducing her to come to the refectory, the sister placed food before her and retired to a little distance; but still Teresa sat motionless, absorbed in her grief. Then in a vision Sister Anne beheld Our Lord standing before the Saint and looking at her with eyes full of tender compassion. Taking the bread which lay on the table, He blessed it and gave it to her, bidding her eat for love of Him. Courage and hope returned to Teresa's heart; the Master had not forsaken the work that He had inspired. Next day she sent word to all the houses of the Reform to redouble their prayers and penances, writing at the same time to the King to implore his help.

The authorities, deceived for a time, were beginning to see where the truth lay. The calumnies of the friars of the Mitigated Rule were proved false. After long and weary waiting a brief was published withdrawing all the houses of the Reform from the government of the Mitigated Order. Shortly afterward Pope Gregory XIII decreed that the friars and nuns of the Primitive Rule should be united in a separate Province governed by a Provincial of their own choosing. Teresa was set at liberty; the Reform was saved.

Chapter 12

THE END OF SORROW

"Our Lord said to me one day: 'Thinkest thou, My daughter, that meriting lies in fruition? No, merit lies only in doing, in suffering and in loving.'" —*St. Teresa*

AT the end of June, 1578 St. Teresa, in obedience to the order of the Provincial, set out on a last visitation of her convents. At Malagon she was laid up with an attack of paralysis, but as soon as she was able to move, continued her journey. At Toledo she fell ill again, but refused to rest. "I am so used to suffering," she said, smiling, "that I can bear it and still go on." After a week of weary travelling in a rough cart over mountainous country she reached Segovia; it was mid-August before she came to Valladolid, where she was again so ill that her life was despaired of.

But new foundations were being asked for in several places, and as long as the Saint had life and breath she must be about her Master's busi-

ness. At Burgos there were trials without number. The Archbishop, after having given his consent to a foundation, suddenly drew back and
opposed the project. Teresa was begged to come
herself and try what she could do. She was in
a burning fever, but would not on that account
delay. "Go, My daughter, and fear nothing," her
Divine Master said in answer to her prayer for
guidance. "I am with thee."

It was bitter wintry weather when the little
party, consisting of the Saint, her faithful Sister
Anne of St. Bartholomew, her niece Teresita and
Father Jerome Gratian started on their journey.
The floods were out, and the whole country
under water. The nuns had to get out of the
cart and walk, or rather wade, through the icy
stream, for the road had altogether disappeared.
It was Teresa, under the burden of her sickness
and her seventy years, who encouraged them and
kept up their hearts; but presently her foot
slipped, and she was nearly carried away by the
torrent. "Ah, Lord!" she cried with loving famil-
iarity, "why do You put such difficulties in our
way?"

"Do not complain, My daughter," was the
answer; "it is thus I treat My friends."

"Ah, my Lord," lamented the Saint, "that is
why You have so few."

Presently they were able to get into the carts

again, but these stuck in the mud, which made another long delay. At last in a torrential downpour of rain they reached Burgos, where a noble lady, Doña Catarina de Tolosa, had offered them hospitality. As may be imagined, the journey had not improved Teresa's condition. The Archbishop, approached once more on the subject of the foundation, declared that he would give his consent on condition that the nuns had a good house and means of subsistence; but a house could not be found.

In the meantime, the Carmelites had to go out to church. One day as they were walking along beside a dirty stream, Teresa gently asked a woman who was standing in the middle of the footpath to let them pass. For sole answer the woman called her a hypocrite and pushed her into the gutter. The nuns were very angry, but the Saint bade them take no notice. "The good woman has spoken truly and acted justly," she said; "that is only what I deserve." Another day, when she was kneeling in the church, some men who were passing in a hurry gave her such a push that they knocked her down. Teresa only laughed at her ill luck and made excuses for them.

At last a kind doctor of Burgos, who had been called in by Father Jerome Gratian to prescribe for the Saint, spoke of her to his friend Ferdi-

nand de Malauga, who offered to lodge the little community in an attic near the chapel of the
large hospital of which he was governor. This
proposal, with its promise of privacy, Teresa gratefully accepted, to the regret of Doña Catarina,
who would have retained her holy guests. The
dwelling was poor, but it looked on to the chapel,
and there were the sick in the hospital to visit
and console. The patients could not have enough
of the Saint. "When Mother Teresa is here," they
would say, "all our pains get better; the very
sight of her does us good."

Dr. Aguiar was still searching everywhere for
a house. The only one for sale was described as
most unsuitable in every way, but as soon as
Teresa saw it, she was delighted. The purchase
was therefore concluded, the Archbishop seem-
ing to approve; but as soon as the nuns had
taken possession, he expressed his displeasure,
and it was only after many anxious moments
that his full consent was obtained. A month later
the River Orlanzon, swelled by violent rains,
overflowed its banks and flooded the whole dis-
trict. Trees were uprooted, houses disappeared;
a sea of water surrounded the convent. Teresa,
who had refused to join the crowds of people
who had taken refuge on higher ground, remained
to pray with her daughters. The cold was intense,
for the water had invaded the lower part of the

house and every gust of wind threatened destruction. The nuns were half starving, for what food there was was under water. At last, when all seemed hopeless, the floods began to abate, and the people of Burgos, in great anxiety as to the fate of the Carmelites, came to the rescue. The doors of the house were broken open so that the water might escape, and the rubbish was cleared out.

At the end of August Teresa went to Valladolid, where she had intended to take a much needed rest, but here a new heartbreak awaited her. As Sister Anne afterward said, "God willed that she should have nothing but suffering all along the road." Maria Bautista, her niece and the Prioress of the convent, displeased with the Saint's decision with regard to a difficult family affair, received her with marked coldness. She had been one of the most devoted of daughters, and Teresa's affectionate heart felt her behavior keenly. Little did the young Prioress foresee that it was the last time that she would see her holy Mother's face on earth, or the bitter regret that her little fit of ill humor would cause her in the days to come.

As for Teresa, half dead with weariness and pain, she went on without delay, her only thought being to console her companions in the discomforts they had to endure. At night they reached a miserable inn, where they could get no food. The Saint was faint with weakness, and Sister Anne tried in vain to get some eggs or something that an invalid could eat. Nothing could be procured but a few dried figs, which she brought to Teresa, weeping.

"Do not cry, dear sister," said the holy Mother; "the figs are very good; many poor people have not as much." The next day she was worse, and when she arrived at Alba the Prioress and the nuns, shocked at her appearance, made her go to bed at once. Teresa smiled. "It is true, my dear children," she said, "that I am very tired, but I have not been to bed so early for twenty years." Next day she arose in time for Mass and received Holy Communion. For a few days she insisted on following the community life, but at last had to declare herself vanquished.

They put her in a little room that looked on the chapel, where she lay and prayed in a happy silence. She was near her Lord, and that was all she desired. The sisters succeeded each other before the altar, praying, praying that God would spare that precious life; a heavy sorrow lay like a pall upon the house.

In the sickroom a strange perfume exhaled from the body of the dying Saint, all the more wonderful because the doctors had prescribed rubbing with an ill-smelling oil which they hoped would relieve the pain. Everybody who entered noticed it; the whole room was scented as with jasmine, lilies and roses. Teresa, who felt that the end was near, asked for the Last Sacraments.

It was five o'clock in the afternoon, and the last rays of the setting sun were lighting up the shadows when they brought her the Bread of Life. As she turned to greet her Divine Lord, her face shone once more with that radiant light that her daughters had so often seen while she prayed; she was as one transfigured, young and beautiful as of old. "I die the faithful daughter of the Church," she said, after asking pardon of those who were present for all that might have given them pain, and begging their prayers.

The night was spent in great suffering, though not a murmur of complaint passed her lips. At dawn, Sister Anne of St. Bartholomew, knowing the Saint's love of cleanliness, clothed her from head to foot in spotless linen, and was thanked by a loving and grateful smile. Lying on her side with the Crucifix in her hand, Teresa remained for the rest of the day, silent and motionless, lost in a loving contemplation of her crucified Lord. A supernatural beauty and joy shone from her face; those who were near watched her in an awestruck silence; such a chamber of death seemed to them like the gate of Heaven.

To Sister Anne, who had been Teresa's faithful companion for so many years, the thought of what life would be without her brought an almost unbearable sorrow. As toward evening she raised her tear-dimmed eyes to pray for help and comfort, she beheld in a vision Our Lord surrounded by Angels looking down with loving glance upon Teresa, as Sister Anne had seen Him stand and look once before in the refectory at St. Joseph's. As she gazed, the burden of her grief grew light; a divine consolation filled her heart, and she turned once more toward the bed. Even as she moved, the Saint sighed once or twice softly and entered into the life that is eternal.

So died St. Teresa, and how can that blessed passing be more eloquently described than in the words of the Saint herself?

"How sweet at the hour of death to go before Him whom we have loved above all things! What happiness to think we are not going to a strange country, but to our own country, since it is to the home of that adorable Spouse whom we love so much, and by whom we are so much loved!"

The Last Communion of St. Teresa

If you have enjoyed this book, consider making your next selection from among the following . . .

St. Catherine of Siena. *F. A. Forbes* 6.00
St. Teresa of Avila. *F. A. Forbes* 6.00
St. Ignatius Loyola. *F. A. Forbes* 6.00
St. Vincent de Paul. *F. A. Forbes* 6.00
St. Athanasius. *F. A. Forbes* 6.00
St. Monica. *F. A. Forbes* 6.00
Pope St. Pius X. *F. A. Forbes* 8.00
The Guardian Angels 2.00
Eucharistic Miracles. *Joan Carroll Cruz* 15.00
The Incorruptibles. *Joan Carroll Cruz* 13.50
Padre Pio—The Stigmatist. *Fr. Charles Carty* 15.00
Ven. Francisco Marto of Fatima. *Cirrincione*, comp. 1.50
The Facts About Luther. *Msgr. P. O'Hare* 16.50
Little Catechism of the Curé of Ars. *St. John Vianney* . . 6.00
The Curé of Ars—Patron St. of Parish Priests. *O'Brien* . . 5.50
The Four Last Things: Death, Judgment, Hell, Heaven . . 7.00
Confession of a Roman Catholic. *Paul Whitcomb* 1.50
The Catholic Church Has the Answer. *Paul Whitcomb* . . . 1.50
The Sinner's Guide. *Ven. Louis of Granada* 12.00
True Devotion to Mary. *St. Louis De Montfort* 8.00
Autobiography of St. Anthony Mary Claret 13.00
I Wait for You. *Sr. Josefa Menendez* 75
Prayer—The Key to Salvation. *Fr. Michael Müller* 7.50
The Victories of the Martyrs. *St. Alphonsus Liguori* 10.00
Canons and Decrees of the Council of Trent. *Schroeder* . 15.00
Sermons of St. Alphonsus Liguori for Every Sunday . . . 16.50
A Catechism of Modernism. *Fr. J. B. Lemius* 5.00
Abortion: Yes or No? *Dr. John L. Grady, M.D.* 2.00
Hell Quizzes. *Radio Replies Press* 1.50
Purgatory Quizzes. *Radio Replies Press* 1.50
Virgin and Statue Worship Quizzes. *Radio Replies Press* . 1.50
The Holy Eucharist. *St. Alphonsus* 10.00
Meditation Prayer on Mary Immaculate. *Padre Pio* 1.50
Little Book of the Work of Infinite Love. *de la Touche* . . 3.00
Textual Concordance of/Holy Scriptures. *Williams*. H.B. . 35.00
Douay-Rheims Bible. *Leatherbound* 35.00
The Way of Divine Love. (pocket, unabr.). *Menendez* . . . 8.50
Mystical City of God—Abridged. *Ven. Mary of Agreda* . . 18.50

At your Bookdealer or direct from the Publisher.
Call Toll Free 1-800-437-5876

Prices subject to change.

ABOUT THE AUTHOR

This book was authored by Mother Frances Alice Monica Forbes, a sister of the Society of the Sacred Heart, Scotland.

The future author was born on March 16, 1869 and was named Alice Forbes. Alice's mother died when she was a child, and her father became the dominant influence in her life, helping to form Alice's virile personality and great capacity for work. She was raised as a Presbyterian.

In 1900 Alice became a Catholic. The Real Presence in the Eucharist had been the big stumbling-block to her conversion, but one day she was hit by the literal truth of Our Lord's words: "This is My Body." Only a few months after her conversion, she entered the Society of the Sacred Heart, becoming a 31-year-old postulant. She seems to have received her vocation at her First Communion, when Our Lord kindled in her heart "the flame of an only love."

In the convent, Sister Forbes used her keen intelligence and strong will to make generously and completely the sacrifices that Our Lord asked of her each day. She put great store by the virtue of obedience. Much of the latter part of her life was spent in illness and suffering, yet she was always kind and uncomplaining—a charming person and a "gallant" soul. Throughout her sufferings the most important thing to her was the love of God. She died in 1936.

Mother Frances Alice Monica Forbes wrote many

books, including a series of interesting short lives of selected Saints called "Standard Bearers of the Faith." One of these books, that on Pope St. Pius X, was very highly regarded by Cardinal Merry del Val, who was a close friend of Pope Pius X.

Other works by Mother Frances Alice Monica Forbes include *St. Ignatius Loyola, St. John Bosco: Friend of Youth, St. Teresa, St. Columba, St. Monica, St. Athanasius, St. Catherine of Siena, St. Benedict, St. Hugh of Lincoln, The Gripfast Series of English Readers* and *The Gripfast Series of History Readers*, various plays, and a number of other books.

The above information is from the book *Mother F. A. Forbes: Religious of the Sacred Heart—Letters and Short Memoir*, by G. L. Sheil (London: The Catholic Book Club, 1948, by arrangement with Longmans, Green & Co., Ltd.).